Public Interest Liberalism
and the Crisis of Affluence

Robert D. Holsworth

Public Interest Liberalism and the Crisis of Affluence

Reflections on Nader, Environmentalism, and the Politics of a Sustainable Society

1980

G.K. Hall & Co.   Boston, Massachusetts

Schenkman Publishing Company   Cambridge, Massachusetts

Copyright © 1980 by Schenkman Publishing Company, Inc.

Library of Congress Cataloging in Publication Data

Holsworth, Robert D
  Public interest liberalism and the crisis of
affluence.

  Bibliography: p.
  Includes index.
  1. Consumer protection--United States--Addresses,
essays, lectures. 2. Nader, Ralph--Addresses,
essays, lectures. I. Title.
HC110.C63H64   381'.44'0973   80-22254
ISBN 0-8161-9032-1
ISBN 0-87073-061-4 (pbk.)

This publication is printed on permanent/durable acid-free paper
MANUFACTURED IN THE UNITED STATES OF AMERICA

2157218

To my parents

Contents

Acknowledgments

I want to thank a number of teachers, colleagues, and friends who aided me throughout the writing of this book. John S. Nelson, John Hutt, Lewis Lipsitz, Orion White, and Frank Munger made helpful comments on the initial formulations of some chapters. Scott Keeter, Jane Sloop, Beth and Tom Uhlman, Steve Mastrofski, Jeane Hunter DeLaney, Elliott Kent, Polly Wheeler, and Mary Hulburt gave their support at various stages of the work. Linda Joyce and Anneliese Warriner expertly typed the manuscript. Paul Kress not only provided a chapter-by-chapter commentary on the book's original draft but has encouraged me in my efforts to think sensibly about political affairs for the past five years. Finally, I am grateful to Paul Price who spent innumerable hours with me patiently explaining the strengths and weaknesses of my ideas. I am sure that much of what is valuable in my thinking has emerged from my association with these people. I do, of course, absolve them from any responsibility for the errors and foolishness which might still be contained in the work.

Chapter Six "Recycling Hobbes: The Limits to Political Ecology" originally appeared in slightly different form in the Spring, 1979 issue of *The Massachusetts Review*.

Chapter 1

Introduction

Much of what follows was gleaned originally from an effort to deal with a personal sense of near despair concerning the present state of American politics. The sources of this unease were the tensions that I felt by continuing to speak about politics and the possibility for conscious and widespread change, which I thought to be so needed but found difficult to imagine. Every now and then, a student of mine has suggested that we should not waste our time worrying about others, that we should seek those niches of slack within the system where we can find some measure of personal fulfillment. Often, these are not flippant remarks but reflective comments of young people who are not impressed by the possibilities for improvement that our variety of politics promises and not excited by the life-options which a devotion to the common good presents. On these occasions I have an inclination to respond "you're right"; instead, I get a hold on myself and answer with a standard professional witticism to the effect that you might not be interested in politics, but politics is interested in you.

My unvoiced urge, if I judge my friends and some of my colleagues correctly, constitutes a secret that many of us share who currently speak about politics and tentatively plan to spend the remainder of our lives so doing. As a matter of course, we pursue a politics of the "just barely possible"; more frequently than not, we settle for the lesser of two evils in our political choices, and we struggle against despairing altogether and accepting the premise that the important political battles are already lost. Endeavoring to extend the benefits of the welfare state to those who have been excluded, we tinker with the institutional machinery to secure a minimally decent life for those without independent means. This is obviously an important task, but in the end we know that many of our personal and political needs have been left unfilled.

Coming of political age in the sixties and early seventies, I felt quite differently only a few years ago. Despite America's involvement in a war for which I could discern no convincing justification, I did believe in the im-

minence of positive change, in the birth of a new culture that would undoubtedly exert a salutary influence on American politics and in the formation of a new person who would be less ambitious, less selfish, and
more cooperative than his predecessors in the modern era. Today these
beliefs seem to have been chimeras, delusions shared by the ahistorical
young with some of their overly optimistic elders. The image that showed
us as voyagers on a ship piloting toward the authentic city on earth now
appears with the populace as passenger-victims of a train barrelling
toward extinction. Our scholars rarely employ the language of liberation
and authenticity but speak in the more austere idiom of survival as they
have become sobered by the magnitude of our ecological challenges.

There is a tendency, among those of us who were temporarily encouraged by the sixties and who now write and teach about politics, to
allow this current pessimism to block our rational perception of events. In
distinction to the way things were, the seventies have come under a
blanket indictment as a politically inactive era in which the striving for
positive social change has been replaced by a philosophy of selfishness
and a complete retreat from political involvement. The claim is accurate
insofar as few supporters of the established order appear visibly troubled
about the possible rending of the social fabric, and few members of
anything resembling an alternative culture speak confidently of its eventual ascendance. Massive demonstrations are infrequent, and our
political passions less fevered as the highly charged issues which both
divided and inspired us have receded. Still, not every blossoming of
citizen-initiated reform has withered; at least some of the progressive activism which took root in the sixties has now matured to become a prominent feature of our political landscape. Most noticeably, the enduring
legacy of the movement begat by Ralph Nader in the latter part of the
decade has been the proliferation of public-interest groups in Washington, D.C.—complemented by the formation of hundreds of citizen-action
groups in local communities.[1] Energetic activism has not totally
dissipated, but it is less obtrusive in style and, I think, less challenging to
our traditional social and cultural mores.

Nader, his followers, and those who have adopted his manner of
politics have generated a wealth of commentary throughout the years,
although the range of attention has been relatively narrow and the quality
uneven. Journalists have written a number of popular biographies of
Nader. Some have published well-researched, balanced presentations;
others have seemed intent on canonizing the man; at least one writer has
been equally consumed with demonstrating Nader's kinship to the devil.
Policy analysts, economists, and law professors have published more
rigorously intellectual works in which they have analyzed specific recom-

mendations issued by Nader, especially those regarding the likely effects of regulating more strictly or deregulating certain industries. The conclusions reached in these investigations have been mixed because the evaluation of Nader often depends on the ideological predisposition of the writer. A principal weakness of both journalists and academics has been their failure to address the questions of broader significance which the progress of public-interest reform as a mode of political action should occasion. [2]

Neither journalists, law professors, nor, for that matter, any of us who specialize in writing about contemporary politics have devoted significant time to answering questions such as: How accurate a depiction and explanation of our political condition have Nader and other public-interest reformers provided? Will the politics of public-interest reform serve as an adequate model to meet our political needs in the future? And, if not, what alterations and transformations should be made so that the activities of progressive reformers might in the future become more relevant to our troubles? Perhaps it is distasteful for many of us who thought we had transcended liberalism in the sixties and early seventies to rivet our attention to yet another variant of it, but the risks in not doing so surely outweigh the costs involved. If we are to state precisely why public-interest reform is or is not an appropriate interim or long-term response to the problems besetting the American polity, it is incumbent on us to bring whatever critical acumen we can muster to the analysis of the activity.

This work attempts to respond to the broader questions which the germination and development of public interest liberalism should elicit. My argument will be that Nader has provided a reasonable explanation of *some* elements of our political condition—especially the frequent victimization of consumers. But Nader will not serve as a fully adequate model for progressive reformers in the future because the starkness of his vision is not matched by an equal profundity in his analysis of the internal dynamics of a consumer society. He neither explains the human costs of the hidden victimization which pervades consumer cultures nor articulates a convincing program that would permit us to meet our likely ecological threats. I plan to contend, however, that the inadequacies of a liberal reformism such as Nader's in confronting environmental challenges and the contemporary crisis of affluence should not be construed to mean—as many serious scholars are coming to believe—that we must also abandon democratic norms and embrace authoritarian solutions. [3] We might instead seek to establish a sustainable society through a commitment to more generous principles of distributive justice and through the creation of a politics which nurtures our relational capacities as an alternative to that which endlessly multiplies our consumer satisfactions.

The ensuing chapters begin with an interpretation of the recent historical development of public interest liberalism. This reformist impulse arose in the sixties in response to the evident deficiencies of American pluralism. Chapter Two shows that Nader self-consciously located himself, both in rhetoric and intellectual bent, between the conventional politicians of the era and the radical critics of American society who were increasingly vocal in their condemnation of that society's expressed priorities. In opposition to the former, Nader and his followers regularly excoriated our elected leaders for allowing well-heeled interests to obtain unwarranted political clout at the expense of poorer, less-organized groups. This imbalance of power was most prevalent in relations between producers and consumers. Corporate enterprises had not only blatantly disregarded the health and safety of consumers but had succeeded in using their political influence to ensure that the exploited had no legal claim to redress. Yet despite the critical volleys with which he routinely peppered the Establishment, Nader was also careful to eschew identification with the radical causes of his time. He lived through the sixties without becoming measureably involved in the civil-rights and antiwar struggles. Moreover, his denunciations of socialism were frequently simplistic, and he rarely carefully examined or doubted the values of American society which were repugnant to many of its youthful dissenters. His politics were consistent with those criticisms of American pluralism that demonstrated the practical inequities of interest-group liberalism, but his politics also largely ignored the complaints of those who were dismayed by our lack of community and our proclivity to substitute the criterion of technical efficiency for moral judgment.

Chapter Three is an explication of the ideology which characterizes this middle path taken by Nader and reformers who have followed in his wake. I claim that the popular analysis of liberals as naive optimists who assume that the human condition can be perfected through governmental intervention is inappropriate when applied to Nader. He is more accurately perceived as an heir to that strand of the liberal tradition which considers the life of individual man to be one of constant anxiety, that is, threatened by the knowledge that the unscrupulous will perpetually seek to take advantage of the unwary. Nader's defensive liberalism has been important because it has both effectively sensitized us to the variety of corporate practices which undermine our well-being and has established that organized citizen action can limit, if not prevent, the frequency of these abuses. But since the political psychology of Nader's movement is grounded on the notions that we are primarily maximizers of our material interests and that furthering our interests as consumers is almost always politically reasonable, he confronts a set of practical quandaries that he is unable to resolve successfully. He becomes incapable of speaking about the victimization that we experience as a result of linking our identities to the pursuit of consumer goods; his exhortations to participate become subverted by the passivity which the satiation of consumer desires engenders; and, as is demonstrated in Chapter Four, he is unable to articulate a well-defined, persuasive, and consistent position on environmental matters.

Chapter Four contends that the practical contradictions of Nader's liberal reformism are clearly manifested in his treatment of ecological problems. Two dilemmas are evident. First, since Nader, for pragmatic reasons, has not sought to alter the consumption ethos fostered by American commercialism, he is reluctant to advocate either restrictions on the level of consumption or the reorientation of our lives away from the prevailing ethos—measures which most political ecologists deem necessary. For environmentalists, Nader does not go far enough. Secondly, since Nader is a sensitive liberal who does exhibit a degree of ecological awareness, he is bound to anger those who feel that consumption should be unrestricted. To persons predisposed to think that Nader is unduly paternalistic, the steps that he does take in the area of environmental regulation are further evidence that he goes too far. Both of these charges are the inevitable result of trying to maintain a consumerist position on environmental matters.

Yet achieving consistency about ecological dilemmas is no simple chore. Examined one-by-one, these dilemmas constitute a formidable array of perplexing challenges in population control, pollution control, energy allocation, and resource management. Such challenges become even more bedevilling when the particular issues are conjoined because they then represent a summons to alter the way in which we lead our personal and collective lives. We now seem to face a crisis of affluence which requires that we limit our escalating wants as consumers and tailor our politics to a less optimistic forecast of the possibility or advisability of rapid economic growth. The tendency of mainstream politicians not to acknowledge the potential gravity of these interrelated ecological threats is ample evidence of the difficulty that will be involved in making any directed social transition. Politicians on the right have been reluctant to admit the pressing reality of ecological imbalances, while those with liberal sympathies have also been chary of making the hard political choices that these issues appear to demand. Like Nader, many liberals speak at one moment of the necessity for vigorous environmental legislation but then are reluctant to endorse the politically unpopular measures which might set limits on the consumption behavior of their constituents.

One "radical" answer to our crisis of affluence that has recently gained some scholarly currency assumes that our existing institutions and reformers cannot solve ecological problems. More than one scholar has suggested in the past five years that the establishment of authoritarian governments and the abandonment of cherished democratic practices may be necessary to meet the urgency of environmental threats. I hold that "technological authoritarianism" is neither a particularly novel response nor necessarily the most appropriate one when a society faces a condition in which resources have to be prudently husbanded in order to sustain all its members at a relatively decent level of material existence. Technological authoritarianism, thought by some today to be the best answer to the "limits to growth," was also endorsed by a few thinkers while America was in the process of industrializing—when these limits were taken for granted. Chapter Five is an interpretation of two turn-of-the-century political economists, Simon Patten and Thorstein Veblen, who wrote in reaction to what I term our first crisis of affluence.[4] Patten was a liberal who believed that minor adjustments in a market economy could lead to a sustainable society, while Veblen was the "radical" who came to believe that the problems of liberalism could only be solved by a benevolent authoritarian state. My conclusion posits that Veblen was correct in asserting that the capacity to use resources judiciously will require a more critical perspective on the psychological foundations of business societies than Patten or later liberal reformers have normally adopted. But I also maintain that this capacity should not be developed by accommodating both the organization of production and the structure of our personality to the technological "wisdom of the machine," as Veblen advised.

The first crisis of affluence was muted by the Great Depression and World War II, then deferred in the fifties and sixties when the increase in our productive capacities exceeded the predictions of either Veblen or Patten. To be sure, the fruits of the increase were not distributed equally, and a sizeable portion of the population remained unduly impoverished. The possibility of ameliorating this condition, however, was usually linked to a growing economy and not to the redistribution of benefits within the context of a stationary state. Chapter Six critically examines the argument of some contemporary ecological writings which contends that only authoritarian regimes can restrict the unflagging expansion of the industrial system and cap the ecological irruptions already noticeable. I propose that the arguments of the new elitists can be reversed to accept, in somewhat altered form, the political assumptions of liberalism that were discarded by the "radical" ecologists. At the same time it would be necessary to reject the economic and psychological "givens" which remain at the core of the ecologists' work, even when they are loudly distancing themselves from the liberals with their rhetoric.

I am not certain that a politics that can remedy the defects which I believe to be at the core of the liberal reformism exemplified by Nader and a politics of ecological survival occupy opposite poles on the spectrum of action. The events and perceptions of the seventies ought not to invalidate a concern for community development, a commitment to a more equitable distribution of wealth, and a search to discover activities more worthwhile than our consumer pursuits. In other words, I am not sure that the measures that will allow us to skirt an environmentally-induced political catastrophe will not also aid us in our quests to lead more decent, more humane lives. We may, of course, face a grim era of sacrifice, privation, and bitterness in which leaders attempt, probably unsuccessfully, to extract obedience from the citizenry through the utilization of whatever coercive measures are available. But there is the opportunity, and as of now only an opportunity, to combine limited growth (or perhaps a tangible decrease in our standard of living) with the creation of vibrant forms of social and political existence that will impart meaning to our lives in a more fulfilling manner than the pursuit of consumer goods within the growth economy had yielded to date. It is possible that a confluence of objective events, innovative ideas, and concerned activists will provide the impetus for a politics that is currently only imagined. The final chapter speaks to these frail hopes. The entire work is an attempt to make a contribution to this development.

Chapter 2

Public Interest Liberalism: A Sensible Alternative?

An implicit requirement of people involved in politics is that they be able to present a pithy definition of that activity at appropriate moments. Some college professors in political science provide the rationale for their focus on the distribution of economic benefits in American society by stating authoritatively at the beginning of their courses, "It all boils down to who gets what, when, and how." Eugene McCarthy has expressed a sense of ironical detachment about his vocation in front of various audiences with the remark, "Politics is like coaching football; you have to be smart enough to understand the game but dumb enough to think it is important." Elected officials less sardonic than McCarthy have a favorite summation to which they are especially apt to refer whenever they are speaking to a group of academics, young people, or anyone they imagine to be idealistic and unimpressed by the bargaining skills which comprise their stock-in-trade. They are wont to tell us, "Like Aristotle said, I believe that politics is the art of the possible." This definition has been repeated by politicians of various stripes. Many who have never read a word of the Greek philosopher have repaired to the definition to justify the crassest and most self-serving of compromises; while in the mouths of others, the definition accurately describes the honest and torturous reluctance with which they meekly abandon principles deeply felt and accede to the demands of expediency in order to obtain a partial victory.

Political reformers frequently, for tactical purposes, describe their causes as exercises in the art of the possible. Ralph Nader stressed his pragmatic orientation to convince a potential constituency that the mobilization of energy he advocated would necessarily result in the achievement of tangible gains. Nader had been depicted initially as a sole combatant against the aligned forces of injustice. He was a "Lone Ranger" in Wild West parlance, a David battling Goliath in Biblical metaphor, and—in more conventional American trope—a man fighting city hall. If the citizenry was being ravaged by the silent but steady violence of special interests, at least one man was laboring eighteen hours each day in our behalf. Despite the personal gratification that he might have received from the publicity testifying to his uniqueness, Nader realized that a sustained movement for political reform required more extensive work than that which his own personal endeavors could produce. He publicly repudiated journalistic descriptions which equated his desire to remain a loner in his private life with a similar political motivation. He reminded his interviewers that he was not interested in the "Lone Ranger" image and continually exhorted the populace to take positive action against those who exploited it.[1] Nader's speeches and writings were punctuated by the contention that his undertaking were best complemented by the formation of an active citizenry which could pressure those who routinely ignored the fundamental interests of the public.

By attributing an immediate political relevance to his movement, Nader was also engaged in a self-conscious enterprise to compare himself favorably with the more radical critics of our system's priorities and the countercultural dissenters who had received the bulk of the media's attention. Nader waged a two-front battle during the early years of his activism. He wanted to focus public attention on the pervasiveness of corporate injustice but acted as if success could only be obtained in this task by distancing himself from radical critics who espoused a socialist ideology and from youthful protesters who exhibited a distressing political naivete. While Nader attacked our established modes of economic and political organization for exposing the average person to unnecessary risk on a daily basis, he simultaneously impugned the rationality and tactical acumen of those further to his left.

Recently, speculation about Nader's loss of popularity and probable demise have become newsworthy items. Nader, it is said, has spread himself too thin and become chaffing to a population which has a greater need for moral reassurance than for sermons hailing brimstone. Perhaps this is the case, though I am more inclined to believe that the postmortem is premature and that public esteem for Nader will stabilize at a level for which most of our political figures are still desirous. We can, however, admit that Nader's prestige may be declining somewhat without substantially altering our estimation of his importance. His most significant legacy is the development of a vocabulary of protest and a style of political action which has characterized the most vigorous strand of contemporary, progressive, American political activism and which is likely to persist regardless of any shift in Nader's popularity. His method of describing a matter in which the general welfare is being systematically undermined, publicly denouncing the culprit, and then prescribing a solution has been adopted by citizen groups throughout the states. Some campaigns against nuclear power plants, mobilizations to halt utility-rate hikes, and proposals for fairer and more understandable pricing of pharmaceuticals have their roots in the vocabulary and style of action inspired by Nader.[2]

This chapter interprets the origins and purpose of the public-interest reform movement which Nader begat. The argument is that Nader attempted to stake out a middle-path between those who believed that the system was functioning adequately and those who claimed that American institutions were fast becoming intrinsically bankrupt. This purpose was evident in the nature of the concerns to which he directed his attention, in his public statements of intent, and in his reaction to other forms of activism. I will support this contention by comparing Nader's diagnoses of American society and prescriptions for it with four critiques emanating from intellectual circles during the sixties and early seventies. Nader's position was akin to those who claimed that interest-group liberalism fostered an unjustifiably unequal distribution of power, influence, and material benefits. His criticism, however, was framed in a manner that permitted him to refrain from suggesting that the inequities described were the natural consequences of a capitalist economy. And though Nader occasionally echoed the phrasing of critical academics by speaking of the common good, community control, and ending the tyranny of the experts, his actions exhibited only a partial understanding of these concepts. The conclusion suggests that while Nader has successfully politicized issues which had inexcusably remained off our political agenda, his inability to fathom and to politicize the good reasoning contained in the scholarly criticism of American pluralism and youthful dissent in the sixties has resulted in an unduly narrow and mechanical reading of political possibilities.

The Reasonable Opposition

The public-interest reform movement which began a decade ago under Nader's auspices entered a political arena already crowded with fevered activism. In the late fifties and early to mid-sixties, liberal Americans had gained a critical awareness of the persistence of racial discrimination and were beginning to question the complacent assumption that all was getting better in American society. The explosions in the black ghettoes accented this doubt with unmistakable intensity. By the time Nader was shedding his Lone Ranger image by earnestly seeking recruits to his causes and establishing the quasi-institutionalization of his advocacy in Washington, D.C., opposition to the war in Vietnam had also become increasingly vocal and widespread. Nader was originally located on the periphery of American activism; he did not become centrally involved in either the black struggle or the antiwar movement. Instead he focused his energies on the broader and more amorphous theme of the corporate undermining of the public-interest, and he alleged that few of us were unafflicted by this most basic form of victimization.

Nader's indictment started with the contention that the interests of the public, especially those interests we shared as consumers of goods and services, were routinely disregarded due to the callousness and greed of large corporate enterprises. The basic dilemma of irresponsible business practices was compounded by the insensitivity of political decision-makers; indeed, elected officials and bureaucratic appointees were typically part of the problem. Politicians who were scions of wealth themselves had often been raised in an ideological atmosphere sympathetic to the corporate requests for special treatment. Those of less noble stock had frequently become connected to the corporate interests through their training in law school and in the years thereafter that were spent in law firms defending the perquisites of the corporations. Political involvement had cemented the invidious partnership because many candidates curried the favor of those who could afford generous campaign donations.

The sweetheart relationship between corporate enterprise and the political establishment undermined the possibility that deliberation and debate among the partisans of the parties would terminate with decisions that were the best possible approximation of the public interest.[3] The proceedings inside congressional committees and administrative agencies, in Nader's analysis, were often epiphenomenal in the sense that much of the detailed factual information presented on these occasions had its origins with the lobbyists of industry and reflected the priorities of the corporate agenda. Furthermore, the monopolistic communication system inhibited the effectiveness of those representatives who were predisposed to think of the commonweal in their evaluation of issues. Such representatives were constrained from advancing their position by the paucity of accessible information with which to counter the claims of industry. In an unwitting paraphrase of Marx, the message of Nader's activism was to inform us that the government was serving as the executive committee of the corporate elite.

The methods by which the public interest had been subverted worked with startling efficiency because these methods had gone largely unnoticed by the public. We had settled for symbolic rewards and enthusiastically supported the power structure even while it inflicted physical harm on us. Nader summarized his beliefs about our socialization processes in a comment on a violent blue-collar reaction to some antiwar demonstrators. "The construction workers were a perfectly predictable product of our educational system. They're breaking heads to defend the system, but the system is killing them. . . . They worry about kids destroying the flag but they, their bodies, are being destroyed by industrial practices which take nothing into account but profits. . . . Workers have been corrupted to use the flag as a fig leaf, not, according to my understanding, the purpose of the flag. . . . I would say immediately to the workers, 'Stop this terrible emphasis on symbols. Don't fight over symbols, but over reality'."[4] Blinded to the actual distribution of costs and benefits throughout society, we had, in Nader's mind, lost the capacity to see events plainly and thus diminished the chances of perceiving our best interests.

Nader and those were attracted to his cause believed that an alternative might be counterposed to this grim state of affairs. We needed a political movement that could artfully portray the distance between the symbolic benefits and the reality of political practice, that could challenge politicians who supported this organization of affairs and raise citizen awareness sufficiently so that concerned groups could initiate positive changes. Specifically, the structure of political and economic power might be described in terms of its malevolent human repercussions. Those politicians who were convincingly proved to be puppets attached to corporate strings could perhaps be removed from office while those whose instincts were adjudged to be humane and sensible might have these tendencies supplemented with the hard information necessary to translate their sentiments into legislation. In popular forums the citizenry could be provided with information that detailed the numerous deceptions to which they were daily subjected. Consumers might be taught the organizational and political skills required to alter the deplorable consistency with which their needs were overlooked.

The trick was to combine information dissemination with a program for reform in order to build a movement that could merge analysis with action. True to the spirit of what has been called the pragmatic genius of American politics, Nader utilized words and theories only so far as these contributed to the furtherance of his concrete goals. Nader has always been unimpressed with those whose work did not adroitly bridge the theory-practice chasm. He has expressed this disapproval with remarks such as "there is too much Athens in present day Washington."[5] In the words of one commentator, "He [Nader] deplores work in goverment departments, scholastic institutions, think tanks and study groups that sacrifice action to academic study. He says that such activities 'lessen the sense of urgency and delude people into thinking that they are acting'."[6] This desire for tangible accomplishments has always weighed deeply on Nader. "I'm not an idealist. I think of myself as very practical because I want to be effective. One of the reasons I do what I do is that I feel very strongly the inadequacy of traditional reformers. They don't do their homework. They all get involved with status, egotism and the rituals of publicity. Even the great old muckrakers like Upton Sinclair and Lincoln Steffens did 20% of the job. They didn't follow through by mobilizing a concerned constituency."[7]

Nader did not believe that his cause could be contained within the available channels of oppositional activism. He felt that the labor movement, the traditional adversary of corporate enterprise, had stagnated because the co-opted leadership had grown primarily interested in consolidating its own position of influence. Charging that it was bloated by success, Nader regularly sniped at big labor. His own program of consumer advocacy, he said, could subsist on the amount of money the "labor unions spend for martinis at Miami Beach."[8] But Nader's disgust with the course of the labor movement did not lead him to walk into the camp of the New Left. When he wanted to prosecute his case against corporate enterprise, he spoke as if he was sympathetic with radical activism by stating, "When you talk about violence don't talk about the Black Panthers, talk about General Motors, there is a total breakdown of law and order with respect to corporate crime."[9] But if statements like this were pitched in a radical key, Nader scrupulously moderated his tone when he defined the ideological nature and purpose of his enterprise. "It's a disservice to view this as a threat to the private enterprise system or big business. . . . It's just the opposite. It's an attempt to preserve the free enterprise economy by making the market work better; an attempt to preserve the democratic control of technology by giving government a role in the decision-making process as to how much or how little safety products must contain."[10]

The efforts Nader displayed to insulate himself from the taint of radicalism were far more extensive than were required by a reformer's need to achieve credibility within the limits of American political discourse. He not only denied radical intent by professing allegiance to the free enterprise system but utilized the negative connotations with which socialism is imbued in America to disparage his corporate adversaries. He first maintained that socialism was one of two unpalatable conditions which could only be avoided by implementing his proposed reforms. "Unless the challenge of corporate reform is undertaken . . . this country will be headed toward a choice between a corporate state or a socialist state."[11] On other occasions, he and his followers did not bother to make a less than subtle distinction and combined the two polarities by uniting corporatism with the bogeyman of socialism—in lieu of employing the technically correct term of state-capitalism. "The system," as described by Nader, "is a corporate socialism hiding behind the myth of competitive enterprise. . . ." Mark Green told the *New York Times* recently, "When Nader thinks of socialism he doesn't think of Lenin but of Paul Rand Dixon."[12] Even when, years later, his own proposal for consumer cooperatives echoed a Fabian idea of decades past, Nader eschewed the role of political educator and said little to alter the prejudicial conceptions of socialism held by many Americans.

Besides stressing his bona fides as a free-enterprise man, the judicious Nader was also careful not to be identified with the tactical excesses of the sixties' activists or with what he considered to be the irrationality of the counterculture. One of the principal questions raised about Nader during these years was directed at his public invisibility on the questions of poverty, civil rights, and Vietnam. His supporters have usually defended him on this count by arguing that Nader employed a conscious economy of political attention, devoting his scarce resources and limited time to matters in which a surfeit of activity was not already noticeable. "He tries to pick his issues carefully. For example, he feels strongly about the health hazards of cigarettes, but he has not taken up the cause because he feels that other people are already doing a good job of publicizing the peril and seeking reform. Similarly, he is personally opposed to the war in Vietnam, but he has declined offers to add his name to anti-war protests, lest he spread himself too thin."[13] But Nader's distaste with the protestors' life style, his lack of sympathy for some of their goals and his revulsion at their tactics might have prompted his reluctance as much as his desire not to be a superfluous addition to a well-stocked movement. At the very least, Nader's pragmatic rationale for avoiding outward cooperation was reinforced by a more basic gut-level negativity. Responding to a query about his lack of visible empathy with other dissenters, Nader once answered: "They can't get it through their heads that they're on the sidewalk but I'm catching it on a more basic level. What is more intimately involved with civil rights and poverty than the invisible violence of corporations? Who do they think gets cheated, diseased, crippled and generally screwed if not the minorities and the poor."[14] In Nader's evaluation, those who took to the streets carrying placards demonstrated more of an interest in boosting their egos than in actually aiding the people or movement they were ostensibly supporting.

This animus toward the dissenters and the forms of oppositional politics in the sixties was notably manifested in the youthful recruits to Nader's cause. The Raiders were not selected from the ranks of vocal protestors but arrived well-groomed and serious from the classrooms of the Ivy League. They shared their mentor's desire to merge analysis with practical reform. According to Jack Newfield, "The Raiders are not New Left types and are quick to criticize the SDS revolutionaries for being too ineffectual, too theoretical and too irrational. Like their leader, the Raiders try to be personally and culturally conventional."[15] They quickly adopted Nader's work habits, laboring for extended hours in the recesses of administrative agencies, trying to scrutinize the latter's normally secretive methods of operation. One can hardly imagine Nader and his purposeful gadflies joining Norman Mailer and his troupe of "revolutionary alchemists" as they marched to levitate the Pentagon.

The youthful critics of the system, from Nader's perspective, were painfully inattentive to plying the art of the possible. If Nader deliberately utilized an economy of political action, he thought the countercultural dissenters were guilty of a disturbing profligacy. He believed that they frequently channeled their energies into activities which were not politically constructive or socially beneficial. They spent too much time cursing the system, listening to music, and getting high on marijuana or some other hallucinogen. When they did engage in political activity, their tactics, according to Nader, were misguided. The occasional resort to violence was ultimately counterproductive because it only made the supporters of the established order that much more adamant in their defense. The more frequent tactical miscalculation was the dissenters' willingness to battle the Establishment through an exchange of symbols. Although thousands of protestors might be gathered together in one place, the tendency was to fill the afternoon with inspirational speeches which heightened the level of general indignity but which made little or no provision for what Nader believed was the more important chore of lobbying the "real" sources of power.

Nader's desire to distinguish himself from more radical protestors was understandable, and his criticism of the alternative culture's politics (or lack thereof) described genuine weaknesses. Yet one cannot help being uneasy with the manner in which these criticisms were posed. Nader's disdain was expressed too facilely, bespeaking a failure to understand the very real distress that was often articulated in so garbled a manner. He typically insisted that the youthful dissenters be more precise in their talk of political remedies and possible alternatives. "Young people ask: 'Is the system sick?' We can ask them: 'What is your prescription?' "[16] But to argue that everyone, especially the young, should be able to connect their social diagnoses with the appropriate political medicine is to issue a demand that is both politically simplistic and too exacting to be warranted. The rebelliousness prevalent in the sixties should have, at the very least, invited from Nader some reflections on the failure of a relatively affluent society to elicit the loyalty of its upcoming generation. His call for a prescription was equivalent to a doctor telling a patient who knows that he is ill but cannot specify exactly where and precisely how he hurts to "heal thyself."

By reacting so bluntly to the manifestations of youthful rebellion, Nader managed to avoid responding to people such as Paul Goodman and Sheldon Wolin who maintained a critical visage but still realized that we needed to consider the stated need to build alternative communities seriously. By minimizing the relevance of the young to his construction of political reality, Nader also slighted the relevance of their belief that we ought to alter the habits of market individuality even if this meant experiments with building creative space outside the principal institutions. The task for Nader was to hold the system to its promises, not to disturb the foundations of its social and institutional practices. In branding those who did not share this perspective as irrelevant grumblers and malcontents, Nader exhibited his talent for connecting diagnoses of American society to plausible solutions that could be articulated in the halls of Congress—even though such solutions might be purchased at the expense of neglecting to acknowledge some of the deeper issues which pervade American society.

Theory and Practice: Nader and the Criticisms of American Pluralism

The sixties was a particularly fertile decade for political criticism as well as political activity—especially criticism of American pluralism, revisionist democracy or interest-group liberalism, depending on how one labeled our dominant ideology. Although the attacks on our methods of conducting politics were at times confined to themes as narrow as the presidential years of John Fitzgerald Kennedy or the failure of Lyndon Johnson's Great Society programs, the critiques were frequently broader in scope. The intent of the more inclusive works was to explain and criticize the assumptions which undergirded the contemporary operation of American democracy. Dissenting scholars and journalists were opposed specifically to the twentieth-century revision of democratic theory which began by postulating that not every individual could actively participate to influence the government equally and ended with the assertion that a good measure of citizen apathy conduced to the benefit of the entire society.[17]

The initial assumption of revisionist democratic theory—that rational participation by a majority in a large-scale society was improbable—had been coupled with the fearful prediction that if the masses did participate directly, they were likely to follow demogogues of profoundly antidemocratic sentiments. In this account, interest-group liberalism had emerged in industrial democracies as a more realistic and less dangerous mode of political organization than others which relied on mass mobilization. Instead of foolishly striving to implement the impossible, decisions were reached through a bargaining process among the representatives of sundry organized groups. According to its proponents, this modification of the classical democratic idea adequately served the needs of a pluralist society because we all received a share of the benefits (or exactly what we would have desired through active participation) while the sobriety and democratic leanings of our leaders mitigated the potential hazards of antidemocratic mass movements. Both conservatives and liberals fit under this ideological umbrella, not because they propounded the same beliefs, but because the principal differences among them was "to be found in the interest groups with which they identify."[18]

The critical reactions to the workings and justifications of revisionist democracy published by journalists, policy analysts, economists and philosophers in the sixties took two general forms. The first claimed that interest-group liberalism did not function as benignly as its supporters alleged. This position stressed the failure of contemporary American democracy to represent the underprivileged adequately and suggested that a redirection of our policy orientation ought to be our principal political aim. A second group of writers extended the critique to maintain that in the unlikely event interest-group liberalism could ever work to mirror its justification, this version of democracy would remain irretrievably flawed. Unremitting in their condemnation of our policy misdirections, these scholars argued that modest political improvements would be unlikely to ameliorate the anomic social conditions which they believed to be a consequence of our market individuality and technocratic mode of organization. Nader's work almost invariably centered on critiques of the first sort while ignoring the arguments presented by the other group of writers.

PRIVATE POWER AND PUBLIC MATTERS

The critics who focused primarily on what they considered inappropriate policy outcomes challenged the reigning empirical assumptions of interest-group liberalism. They argued that not every salient social grouping was included within our complex of pressure organizations and that well-organized, highly effective groups overrepresented wealthy corporate interests. The pluralist ideology had not fostered an acceptable distribution of benefits but had instead legitimated the silencing of consumers, the neglect of the poor, and the control of the governmental agen-

da by the well-heeled interests. The political task was to discover the implement the methods by which the stranglehold of corporate America on
the political system could be loosened so that the government might be
more responsive to the interests of the less highly organized.

Yet writers who espoused this line of thinking did not necessarily agree
on a solution to the problems that had been described. Policy recommendations issued from this perspective exhibited two general tendencies. One
was to propose that interest-group influence be made more equitable by
institutionalizing the access of the traditionally underrepresented. The
plan was to keep the interest-group system intact but attempt to alter the
outcomes by ensuring that representatives of the poor, the racial
minorities, and consumers were included in the deliberations. A second
recommendation put forth by writers further on the left of the political
spectrum maintained that the priorities of the interest-group system could
not be reversed by adjustments within the prevailing order. Commentators of this persuasion claimed that the inequities of American
pluralism were bound to persist unless the American economy was
reorganized along socialist lines.[19]

Nader has been well-attuned to the ability of corporate enterprise to
establish the rules of political discourse and prevent the institutionalization of a consumer voice. He has labored to reduce the influence of large
corporations by maintaining a countervailing consumer presence in the
capitol. Moreover, he has encouraged the formation of local cooperative
groups that will actively challenge anticonsumer practices by arguing
before the appropriate administrative boards. He has contended that we
need federal chartering of corporations and national standards for corporate practices in order to ensure that those states which impose appropriate restrictions do not experience an industrial exodus. He has also
been generally supportive of movements designed to sever the financial
connection between legislators and corporations.[20]

Nader's views on political economy, however, were much closer to
those who spoke of altering the balances within the established system
than to writers who adopted a more radical stance. His equation of the
consumer interest with the public interest has been the conceptual means
by which Nader and other public-interest activists have been able to be
stridently critical of corporate influence without becoming officially committed to a radical political economy. We have already heard Nader argue
that his credentials as a poverty fighter are impeccable because the poor
are more frequently subjected to consumer deceptions. His belief and his
concern are obviously genuine, but still it is a concern for the poor because they happen to be victimized qua consumers, not primarily because

they happen to be impoverished. This is a well-intentioned outrage with the practices that exploit those who can least afford the loss, but it is also a stance that has allowed Nader to skirt the politically sensitive question of whether those scholars who utilize a class analysis of American society are correct in their assessment that our economy requires a marginal economic class for its periodic cycles of expansion and contraction.

SYMBOLIC POLITICS AND MATERIAL BENEFITS

Some writers who have criticized the unequal distribution of material benefits in American society have tried to explain why the disadvantaged members of the populace have acquiesced to this state of affairs. A prevalent interpretation of citizen silence suggests that actually two kinds of benefits, material and symbolic, are distributed to the citizenry. The powerful are said to pocket the limited material payoffs, while the rest of us are forced to settle for symbolic rewards. In Murray Edelman's words, "We can show that many business regulations and law enforcement policies confer tangible benefits on the regulated businesses while conveying only symbolic reassurances to their ostensible beneficiaries, the consumers."[21] The kernel of the argument is the contention that while all of us do not receive the real material benefits that politics can bestow, we do receive some compensation (albeit different in kind from that garnered by those entrenched in the bastions of privilege) and that symbolic reassurances are usually sufficient nurturance for the powerless.

The notion of symbolic politics, however, is so imprecise that two discrete ideas are conflated into what has become a catchphrase in academic political science. The most simple conception of symbolic politics merely claims that benefits are distributed unequally and the citizenry remains unaware of the degree to which it is "getting screwed" because of our leaders' adroitness in masking fundamental inequities. A more complex interpretation of this notion posits that citizens have actually internalized the norms of an elite-dominated society, and that we accept society's outcomes because, to a large degree, we accept the rules by which the society operates.

The consequences for political action differ according to which conception of symbolic politics is implicitly accepted. If the first interpretation is thought appropriate, reformers will concentrate on presenting information to the citizenry that will destroy our leaders' claims to be acting benevolently. But if the other interpretation of symbolic politics is thought to portray reality more accurately, progressive political action requires strategies that will challenge the established system of distributing benefits as well as demand a bigger and better slice of pie for the disadvantaged.

Nader, as we saw above, has admitted the pervasiveness of symbolic manipulation but has usually not considered the relevance of the second interpretation. He appeals to citizens by publicizing a body of assertions and findings about the workings of American politics which he hopes will destroy the image world of the system's apologists. Nader has succeeded in convincing many citizens that his estimation of corporate enterprise is accurate through an extraordinarily clever selection of examples and because his movement has coincided with a series of events that undermined popular confidence in our institutions and leaders. Yet just as with his argument in the matter of political economy, Nader had defined the consumer as the quintessential victim of symbolic politics and thus defined away the need for attending to criticisms which endorse distributive principles antithetical to those which are followed in a state-capitalist nation.

THE COMMUNITARIAN FAILING

Critics of contemporary liberalism with a philosophical bent often argue that its policy failings are the predictable outcomes of its inadequate psychological underpinnings. They maintain that the prevailing asocial definition of rational behavior in pluralist societies—a definition that characterizes us as short-term maximizers of material interests—is an incomplete understanding of human complexity and an inadequate foundation for responsible politics. This individualized proposition about human nature theoretically denies (or at least considers inconsequential) the existence of natural bonds between persons and systematically depreciates the worth of public, cooperative action. A society whose practices are predicated on this comprehension of human drives is likely, according to the critics, to exhibit widespread manifestations of social anomie because the communal side of our personalities is routinely repressed. A responsible politics is said to be precluded because—as long as citizens participate only to further their economic condition—conceptions of politics animated not by self-interest narrowly construed but by a concern for the public good are necessarily disregarded.[22]

Writers who have disputed the psychological assumptions of liberal utilitarianism usually opt for an alternative understanding of humankind which emphasizes the social nature of our beings. In this interpretation, we are people intimately connected to one another who reach our full maturity through interactions which acknowledge and deepen our natural bonds. Ideally, we would organize our work-lives so that we could select the goods to be produced and the methods of production. We would organize our social space to optimize our chances of meeting congenially with others. And we would organize our political communities so that we could participate in making the decisions that are important for the direction of our lives. The purpose of public action implied in the communitarian perspective is distinct from the political understanding of American pluralism. Instead of only maximizing our particular economic interests, we deliberate about a common good that is greater than the sum of its individual parts and in the process restrict and perhaps civilize the quantitative self's multiplying desires.[23]

Nader has adopted the tone of the communitarian analysis while deleting much of the content. Specifically, he speaks of the common good, the need to further the public interest, and the necessity for a community-oriented politics. But the actual makeup of this common good, however, is once again usually limited to the interests we share as consumers of goods and services. In his magnum opus interpreting the course of American history, the historian Daniel Boorstin claims that there was a perceptible shift in the twentieth century in the nature of communities that Americans formed. As American retail industry expanded and disrupted the local economy of neighborhoods, and as advertising commenced to educate us to the requirements of this burgeoning new sector, we substituted "invisible communities of consumers" for the bonds of neighbors that had been split asunder. Nader has become the untitled protector of these invisible groupings, and though he has performed a worthwhile service for consumers, we should be wary of echoing Boorstin and unreflectively joining the terms "community" and "consumers."[24] To be involved in a genuine community implies a history of face-to-face relationships, a history of shared joys and burdens, and a history which generates a complex set of supportive actions in moments of distress. To suggest that the sharing of similar consumer desires constitutes a sufficient condition for the establishment of a community is really to substitute a new meaning for the concept by draining it of its experiential richness.

THE TYRANNY OF THE EXPERTS

A final deficiency of American pluralism noted by its critics has been the increasing tendency to define political matters as problems to be solved by increasing the use of expertise. The consequences generated by this phenomenon are said to be the augmentation of corporate power and a diminution of our personal competence and faculties of moral judgment and political discernment. In its most prosaic appearance, the reliance on expertise in political decision-making enhances the power of special interests because a principal source of their influence is the plethora of information and "expert" testimony which they can readily offer on matters relevant to the stabilization of their profit margins. A commonplace of American political science now asserts precisely this by telling us that the power of lobbyists emerges from their capacity to present reliable information in digest form to those whom they wish to influence. The control of administrative agencies and regulatory commissions by the very businesses they were designed to regulate was one outcome of the near monopoly that corporations had on the information critical to the operation of the agencies.

Writers who have addressed the theme of the "technological society" have found the pervasiveness of expertise to illuminate a more profoundly worrisome condition than is outlined by the description of corporate influence over administrative decisions. In the words of Langdon Winner, "The full range of technological circumstances in society tends to establish the central agenda of problems politics must confront. It also determines, to a great extent, the nature of solutions to these problems well in advance of any real act of political deliberation."[25] In a highly industrialized society, maintenance of the existing systems of transportation, communication, and manufacturing are almost necessarily first-order political priorities. Since the *maintenance* of these systems is endemically a technical dilemma, the majority of citizens will not be able to participate in the body of political affairs. Furthermore, once the maintenance of the technological system is accepted as a given which cannot be questioned, we also foreclose public discussion regarding the desirability of paying the social costs that the process of repair will necessarily entail. For instance, maintaining an efficient transportation system in an area in which both the population and the number of cars are rapidly increasing might require widening the existing roads and freeways. The consequences of this expansion will be felt not only by those whose homes are to be demolished but by everyone residing in this vicinity. Yet it is only in exceptional cases that considerations of the economic and social effects of the expansion will be taken into account when making the decision to keep vehicular efficiency at its present rate. "Technical systems become severed from the ends originally set for them and, in effect, reprogram themselves and their environment to suit the special conditions of their operation. The artificial slave gradually subverts the rule of its master."[26] The technical apparatus originally designed as a means to facilitate the implementation of human choices has now become an end to be preserved at all costs—independent of our collective judgments.

The potential for ameliorating the abuses of expertise in a technological society and the methods conducive to this end vary according to the description of the malaise. If the problem is narrowly conceived to be a corporate monopoly on the information presented to political decision-makers which fleshes out in the utilization of technologies injurious to the welfare of the public, the obvious response is trust-busting. This is achieved by discovering methods to ensure that alternative sources of information are institutionally represented, by fragmenting the composition of the regulatory commissions by seating those with constituencies traditionally opposed to the excesses of corporate influence, and by publicizing the effects of lobbying so that informed citizens can similarly pressure their elected officials. But if the commentary avers that technology possesses a logic of its own to which we accommodate our political decisions and personal life-styles, the potential for a remedial politics is improbable and the methods of retooling imprecise. Marcuse urges indiviuals to voice a "Great Refusal"; Habermas writes of the possible formation of "communicative competence" which will be characterized by a revitalization of practical reasoning among the citizenry; Winner exhorts us to adopt a strategy of "epistomological Luddism" so that we might "disconnect crucial links in the organized system for a time and study the results."[27] All are reasonable propositions but hardly capable at present of inspiring a transformation equivalent to the bleakness of the descriptions.

Nader's politics have once again echoed the broad phrasing of the critique while leaving conveniently unmentioned the actual content that cannot be easily assimilated to his pragamatic orientation. Vociferous denunciations of the tyranny of the experts have marked a number of his campaigns. On one side of the coin, he simply means that professional associations utilize the political influence that their status naturally accords them in order to insulate their memberships from market forces in a manner eventually detrimental to the public interest. Nader and other public-interest workers have advocated that professionals such as doctors and lawyers be permitted and encouraged to advertise in order to foster open competition in their pricing. They contend that an occasional discount special on gall bladder removals pushed by a huckstering physician could be no worse than the malfeasance that has previously hidden behind a veil of ignorance. The result would be to let a scheduling of prices be engraved on professional shingles and ensure quality control by the sheer quantity of information available to consumers.

On the other side of the coin, Nader's denunciation of the tyranny of the experts expresses his belief that the current utilization of expertise has been unjustifiably skewed to benefit corporate enterprise. He repeated the assertion in many of his study group reports that key regulatory positions in government were staffed by people who shuttled back and forth between the administrative agencies and the firms that were supposedly being regulated. A number of his political campaigns have attempted to balance this seesaw of expert partisanship. He has encouraged "whistle blowing" by public-spirited employees of corporations whose practices are detrimental to the consumer interest, and he has supplemented these exhortations with efforts to protect the job security of those whose primary loyalty is to the general and not the corporate will. The development and institutionalization of public-interest law was an attempt to reduce the influence of Washington lawyers whose clients were major corporations. His recruiting trips at various law schools across the nation for his equal justice movement (requesting that prospective graduates pledge a certain percentage of their yearly income to public-interest law foundations) is an endeavor to institutionalize the principle of equal expertise.[28]

Nader's actions against the tyranny of the experts have infrequently, however, penetrated sufficiently deep to consider the question of whether we have allowed technical criteria to impinge unnecessarily on what are primarily moral and political questions. By maintaining that the trouble with the use of expertise is that the experts are not sufficiently partisan, or that they are partisan instead of nonpartisan, Nader has accurately portrayed an important hindrance to the establishment of fair government. But Nader has not realized that his principle of balancing expertise to contribute to the public interest can have the unanticipated effect of maintaining a subtler tyranny. So long as most political questions are viewed in legal or scientific terms, much of the general population will be forced to remain politically silent. The problem with Nader's perspective is not so much that it is wrong, but that it can lead us to become too complacent with what in reality is only a partial victory, and thus disguise the perpetuation of a process constricting the range of humanly meaningful choices.

Reasonableness and Its Costs

The purpose of public interest liberalism as originally developed by Nader was to provide a reasonable alternative to politics-as-usual in American society without advocating the necessity of radical upheavals. To those who professed to be satisfied with the organization of political and economic affairs, Nader meant to rattle their complacency by describing a series of risks to which consumers were routinely subjected. To those who spoke of problems in American society from their seating in academic chairs, Nader argued that he not only recognized issues but was centrally engaged in the practical struggle for amelioration abjured by most academics. To the young who were outspoken in their condemnation of American society, Nader issued a challenge that they prove their relevance in a contest of pragmatism. Because he could link his diagnosis of societal ailments with working prescriptions for their alleviation, Nader's presumed tactical superiority became the validation for his entire politics.

A principal strength of Nader's activism has been his capacity to fit into the mainstream of American politics without diminishing his stridency and sense of outrage. He has wielded a critical blade that has retained its edge despite years of work in a city that normally blunts the acuity of its political residents. Nader can chat amiably with liberal congresspersons about upcoming legislation and has been instrumental in promoting former members of his entourage into second-level governmental positions (better for them to be seated than corporate designates). Still he is vigilant in his watch that his former associates not mistake kowtowing to the special interests for pragmatism. This resistence to conforming forces is today evidenced fifteen years after his emergence as a public figure as he upbraids ex-aides who have entered government seemingly to lose their single-minded devotion to the public interest. His talent for being critical but pragmatic has allowed Nader to gain a serious hearing in Congress and not be relegated to impotent moaning about the influence of the "Military-Industrial Complex."

Naderite reformers and other public-interest advocates have achieved real gains for the public through their persistent demand that society function more democratically than it recently has. Also, by insisting that the consumer interest be represented, Nader has been instrumental in adding another factor to our political calculus that inexcusably had been excluded to our political agenda. While he has yet to succeed in establishing a Federal Consumer Protection Agency, Nader has contributed to the enactment of much legislation, and the effects of his indictments have been noticeable throughout the states. Whereas fifteen years ago the political delegates of corporate enterprise were often handed carte blanche in directing the affairs of regulatory agencies, these administrative boards currently submit to public scrutiny and occasionally have their memberships balanced by representatives of other constituencies. One significant measure of his influence is the anticipation of Nader-like reactions and the interest taken by corporations in public relations to refute the gist of Nader's allegations.

Nader has exhibited a rare sensitivity to the malfunctioning of the system as it ideally operates, especially when the lever of corporate power is not balanced by a countervailing exertion of consumer rights. His experiences have provided him with a measure of political savvy which political novices rarely possess and he knows how to apply the knowledge he has gained to further his ends. If the political arena is primarily seen as the battleground on which the exercise of corporate power over consumers will either be limited or given full sway, Nader and his followers should be perceived as some of our most talented political infighters. The shortcoming of his methods and understanding of politics is that it is terribly difficult for the Naderites to extricate themselves from the ongoing fisticuffs and recognize the significance of problems not directly related to their definition of political reality.

By describing Nader's reactions to the activists of the sixties and comparing his politics with the writings of scholarly critics of American society, I have not intended to imply either that these two groups were united in theory and practice or that they were always more insightful than the Naderites. The practices of the youthful dissenters were often inchoate, and their limited attempts at theory formation could be endorsed by rigorous thinkers only with significant qualifications. The former lacked a solid grounding in history; their tactics were naive if not destructive; and slogans such as "do your own thing" could be neatly accommodated within the dominant ideology. My intention through such a comparison was to extract some common tendencies frequently expressed by those who occupied the scholarly groves and peoples' parks that Nader ignored. These similar concerns centered on the distribution of wealth in American society, a felt need to build more communal settings for our lives, a dissatisfaction with our lives as consumers, and a belief that we ought to recapture our sense of personal competence in the face of technological omnipotence.[29] While public interest liberalism may represent an improvement on politics-as-usual, and while no one else may have viable answers to the questions which Nader has been reluctant to address, those who feel that Nader is a valuable political figure should also recognize the alternatives that he has not pursued.

A typical method of denigrating persons and activists who raise issues and speak about possibilities not easily assimilated to the dominant political mores is to label them utopian and to suggest that they are "in" this world but ultimately not "of" it. The implication of this charge is that the movement they encourage is really antipolitical and religious in nature. While they speak of imaginary, more perfect societies, the real world of human affairs—the world of sweat and blood in which men and women live and die, the world in which people are exploited, and the world in which this injustice undermines the potential nobility of the human race—proceeds untouched. Like religious prophets, these activists are scorned by the more pragmatic because they seem to overlook injustice in its grotesque present forms in order to search for a better life in the afterworld or, so it seems, in a world never to be. Against this, reformers who deal with the system as it presently stands—who recognize the necessity for compromise and who don't confuse what ultimately ought to be with what can be in the near future—are said to be more attuned to the sufferings which comprise the human condition.

Perhaps this is true, and those who criticize Nader for being too much "in" this world and not detached from it are misguided. Perhaps we should take a long look at the public opinion polls and proffer no remarks about the potential of political action that cannot be substantiated without reference to Mr. Gallup's latest findings. But it just may be that the art of the great and innovative political reformer entails more than a mechanical outlook on political possibilities. The art of the possible can be seen as a dialectical exercise. The best practitioners of Aristotle's dictum will realize that political virtuosity is not defined only by a clever accommodation to existing norms but in an imaginative reordering of the political world that first teases out, then illuminates, and finally carries into the realm of the possible, those probabilities that had been outside our standard definition of reality.[30] It is likely that the successful resolution of the pressing dilemmas of the contemporary age with which Nader and other progressive reformers have yet to grapple will require this sort of imagination.

Chapter 3

Defensive Liberalism and Nader's Grim World

We are quickly becoming a nation of skeptics. The revelations of fundamental and pervasive corruption among our political leaders have led not only to the expected commitment to kick the rascals out, but also to a questioning of the very worth of political activity. Researchers today uncover political disaffection and skepticism toward authority in eight-year-olds. I recently listened to a bemused father tell how his three-year-old son, Alexander, requested that his standard bedtime fare of stories about American folk heroes be interrupted in order that he could be told the tale of Tricky Dick. Historically, Americans have been political kibitzers and usually not rabid participants. Now, however, even the modicum of interest necessary to make kibitzing an interesting pastime appears to be waning.

Despite confirming what a number of critics on the American Left have been saying for years, it appears that within the excessively narrow confines of American political argument, the revelations of corruption have most adversely affected the orthodox progressive and liberal politician. To be sure, a Republican president was removed in 1976 and a preponderantly Democratic Congress elected in both 1976 and 1978, but our animus has today been deflected from particular individuals to become a more general distrust of the governmental intervention that is characteristic of American liberals. Although a number of liberals still retain electoral clout, the new breed of politicians speaks of reorganizing bureaucracies along the lines of efficiency and removing chiselers from the dole. Wars against poverty and inadequate housing have been supplemented and sometimes replaced by forays against bigness and bureaucracy. Orthodox liberals are labeled naive, even by fellow Democrats, and are said to have held unduly optimistic hopes during the sixties. Neo-conservatives denigrate the proliferation of social welfare programs as a device to turn us into a society of hospital patients. And almost everyone critically refers to the gargantuan federal administration which liberals are supposed to have foisted upon an unwilling populace.

Liberals, it is said, do not understand that governments cannot provide and guarantee human happiness.

This chapter specifies the ideology which underlies the middle path which Nader's public-interest reform movement represents. My principal aims are to illuminate Nader's assumptions about the nature of man, his condition in the contemporary world, and the purposes of political action. The argument maintains that an examination of Nader's actions demonstrates that the popular characterization of liberals and liberal activists is both misleading and incomplete. Contemporary liberals and their predecessors have not uniformly exuded optimism about the possibilities inherent in political existence and have not been supporters of the notion that a constant increment of progress is a permanent feature of human affairs. Nader is an activist whose work can be said to be a modern-day corroboration of Sheldon Wolin's claim that liberalism is a "philosophy of sobriety, born in fear and nurtured by disenchantment."[1] Nader's activism is motivated by a belief that the pervasive victimization of the ordinary citizen can only be tempered by a politics of self-defense in which we are ever vigilant in respect to the established corporate and governmental powers.

Nader's political stance has been important because he has struck a responsive chord in our personal experiences and effectively sensitized us to a variety of practices that undermine our well-being. But, in keeping with the argument presented in Chapter Two, it is shown that by grounding his analysis and action in our problems as consumers, Nader (despite his many successes) has neither been able to foster the level of sustained popular involvement that he deems necessary nor been able to address some of the more profound victimizations which routinely afflict consumer societies. Concluding remarks suggest that the extraordinary skepticism concerning the worth of politics which we witness today has its sources not only in rampant elite corruption and majority dissatisfaction with social welfare programs, but also in the failure of progressive reformers such as Nader to articulate and implement a conception of politics that can animate enduring political activity throughout the citizenry.

Defensive Liberalism

Liberalism has always maintained a certain elusiveness which has rendered the task of capturing its essence within a pithy definition extremely difficult. The liberal credo has functioned as a promise, a rhetoric, an ethics, and an ideology. It has contained a diversity of meanings, and notions seemingly contradictory have nestled comfortably under its mantle. To obtain a better idea of what I mean by defensive liberalism, it will be useful to schematize some core assumptions of classical and interest-group liberalism and to compare these with the principal components of Nader's politics. Most significantly for the purposes of this study, I want to outline the fundamental postulates of each regarding the nature and potential of man, the nature of man's interactions with other men as conditioned by the physical environment, and the functions, methods, and potential of political action.

Classical liberalism is usually taken to signify a society in which a system of representative government is grafted onto a free-market economic structure. Its leading ideologists were Bentham, the elder Mill, and the nineteenth-century British political economists. All believed that the greatest happiness principle of utilitarianism was most consistently approached in a system where the incentives of the marketplace were operative. Their key assumptions can be noted as follows.[2]

1) Man is basically a utility maximizer, an appropriator, and consumer who seeks to obtain pleasure and avoid pain. While there are various categories of pleasures, most people will seek primarily to accumulate property and wealth because obtaining wealth and power is perhaps the most effective insurance against pain.

2) Since desire is unlimited and since the environment is characterized by scarcity, there will be perpetual competition for both scarce goods and scarce positions of power. Self-interested, atomistic individuals will necessarily bump into each other in a condition where material and psychic securities are finite.

3a) The function of political action is threefold: To protect individuals from each other, to protect individuals from a tyrannical government, and to preserve the free market structure because this ensures a continued incentive for expanded production.

3b) The best method of protection is a system of representative government in which one-man–one-vote is the general rule. But this system should not be instituted unless it is clear that working-class majorities have been "educated" to accept the market structure.

3c) The potential of political action does not go beyond the function of protection of self and preservation of property.

Classical liberalism is not an optimistic philosophy. Man is anxious that he might not overcome the struggle with nature, he is doubly anxious about his relations with other men, and he is worried about the uses of power by those to whom he has granted the authority to preserve the market. Those on top of the system become, in the history of political thought, Marx's driven capitalists who worry about falling into the ranks of the proletariat. The men on the bottom are consigned to labor incessantly without rising from indigence.

If the popular characterization of liberalism as a philosophy of optimism is reflected in liberal political theory, it is most clearly discerned in the writings of post–World War II political scientists who justified revisionist democracy or interest-group liberalism as the proper method of political organization. Whereas pre-war writings were mostly descriptive, political scientists in the fifties and sixties combined the descriptive claim with the legitimizing postulate that America was the good society in action. The core assumptions were:

1) Man is basically a utility maximizer, an appropriator and consumer who seeks to obtain pleasure and avoid pain. In revising what they considered to be the mistaken axioms of classical democracy, these writers frequently remarked that Aristotle was wrong when he considered man to be a "political animal."

2) The physical environment is one of relative abundance, and —given the existence of affluence—competition for the fruits of well-being need not be fierce. The most important desires of most individuals and most groups of individuals can be relatively satisfied if not completely satiated.

3a) The function of political action is to mediate the demands of the interest groups and to protect the citizenry from tyranny.

3b) The best method is that of competition among elites in which voters choose which set will temporarily rule. As long as elite competition prevails, there will be no need to encourage greater participation in the political arena.

3c) The potential of politics is that everyone will be equitably represented and satisfied materially.

We should realize, however, that the expressed optimism of the democratic elitists was not shared by everyone who studied American politics. As mentioned in Chapter Two, many scholars believed this ideology functioned more as a rationalization for a inequitable distribution of goods than anything else. Studies of the presidency concluded that liberal presidents do more to stabilize the corporate economy than parcel out economic goods reasonably. Research about the welfare system held that the expansion and contraction of the relief rolls is often tailored to momentary political exigencies, not to a deeply held belief about the necessity of redistributing wealth. Students of the administrative process maintained that some groups were invariably omitted from the political calculus.[3]

While Nader's defensive liberalism, which he developed in reaction to the workings of interest-group liberalism, was never intended to be a consistent body of theoretical propositions, a number of postulates can be extracted from his actions which distinguish his brand of liberalism from the ones already mentioned.

1) Man is basically a utility maximizer, an appropriator, and consumer who seeks to obtain pleasure and avoid pain.

2) Although the economic condition of society is one of relative abundance in which most people can afford to purchase many amenities, the majority of Americans are constantly victimized by those whose interests as consumers are secondary to their interests in making a profit off other consumers.

3a) The function of political action is to protect the citizenry from tyranny and to protect the interests of consumers.

3b) The methods of the politics of self-defense are: representation in Washington, representation of the public good in private bureaucracies, and widespread participation by consumer-citizens on local levels.

3c) The potential of political action is that citizens will protect themselves from victimization.

In comparison with the liberalism of Bentham, the elder Mill, and the British political economists, Nader shares the belief that man is essentially a consumer and a utility maximizer. The classical liberal believed that because of scarcity and insatiable appetites, men were likely to be regularly victimized by others wanting their goods and desiring power over them. The function of political action was to protect appropriation and consumption, and the best method for so doing was to preserve the sanctity of labor. By allowing the free market structure to function as designed, some advancement against impoverishment can be made. Since Nader (living in an advanced capitalist nation) has assumed that a sufficient supply of goods can be furnished to keep most people relatively satisfied, the problems which arise in this state are those of "surplus victimization." Nader thus differs from the classical liberals in two important respects. The first is his belief that victimizations do not necessarily come from the condition of man in an environment of scarcity, but from the corporate control of the marketplace in a condition of relative affluence. The second, and perhaps more significant distinction, is found in the extent of participation endorsed by each. Mill endorsed universal suffrage but did not think that anything more than a periodic check on our rulers would be necessary. Nader, on the contrary, believes that only a politicized society with consumers vigorously and constantly asserting their own interests can reduce the existing level of victimization.

Both Nader and interest-group liberals concur that man is basically a utility maximizer, yet they hold differing views on the nature of victimization and participation. The latter emphasize the relative abundance of goods and suggest that most people can be relatively satisfied. Nader argues that this is sheer apologetics, because despite relative abundance, corporate America serves up death and danger with increasing regularity. Given this perspective on victimization, the amount of participation endorsed also varies. Nader encourages participation to a much greater degree than would interest-group liberals. While much of Nader's work takes place in the classic interest-group style, he never suggests that the establishment of a public-interest bureaucracy can substitute for and replace direct action as the essential weapon against victimization. This refusal certainly distinguishes him from those who accept the tenets of group theory.

During his political career, Nader has been characterized by more than one description. Journalists are apt to call him a muckraker and claim him as one of their own. Conservative opponents have called him a radical revolutionary, others have accused him of being an elitist, and leftist critics have dismissed him for being a hopeless capitalist. I think, however, that it is as a defensive liberal that Nader is best understood. I do not mean to contend that any semblance of accuracy is lacking in the above description, but only to say that my label explains more precisely the ideology underlying Nader's purpose. It provides us with a fairly consistent outlook on the nature of man (individual satisficer), his condition in the contemporary world (victim), and the function of political action (self-defense) which the other labels, (deprecatory or laudatory) do not furnish. To call Nader a radical is to think that many of Nader's reforms are designed to foster the creation of a new person when they are primarily meant to force the political-economic system to keep its original promises. Yet to dismiss him altogether as a simple adjunct to the capitalist system fails to perceive the critical distance which lies between Nader and the system's apologists in regard to the depiction of the content of everyday life.

The Pervasiveness of Victimization

The principal component of defensive liberalism is its testimony to the frequency of victimization in our everyday experiences. Its proponents seek to inform us that we share these common experiences of being taken or exploited. Throughout the past decade, Nader has exhibited especial adroitness in ferreting out and publicizing those moments of risk to which many of us are exposed daily with little or no conscious recognition of the extent of the risk involved. Time and again he has revealed, often in dramatic fashion, the distance between the idylls of technological society and the day-to-day realities of our lives. He has publicized the gap between the cars advertised and the weapons and death traps that we purchase. He has demonstrated that the appealingly packaged food in the supermarkets may contain the carcinogens which we unknowingly consume. And he has show how the potential for progressive change in American politics is deflected in the antiquated corridors of Congress. Nader has exposed the middle-class underside of technological America and has affirmed what many of us privately felt but could not articulate with such vehemence or defend with such a plethora of information. In so doing, he has become one of our more credible political figures.

An animating force behind Nader's work has been his belief in a direct but often hidden connection between the private pleasures of our everyday life and our public organizations. The impetus behind specific campaigns has been the discovery that the former has been sacrificed because of the action or neglect of some member of the latter. Nader has also attempted to show that the power which the corporate sector of industry holds in the legislative chambers results in a diminution of the enjoyment that we receive as consumers of goods and services whenever the interests of consumers and profit-oriented producers clash. One important component of his strategy has been to bring this recognition quite literally home. Thus we get the curious situation of a Harvard Law graduate writing a monthly column in *Ladies Home Journal* advising housewives of the possible dangers they might encounter while performing their daily tasks.

The idea of victimization describes, according to Nader, the manner in which our everyday lives are affected by concentrated political and corporate power. By constructing a link between the remote and the personal, he endeavors to politicize everyday life, and through his activism, strives to convince the ordinary citizen that the level of victimization and the discomforts now endured can be reduced by altering the organization of our public institutions. The act of demystifying the often obfuscated connections—as much as the particular content of his criticism—has lent Nader his most critical thrust. The whole range of his activites gain continuity and cohesion due to the persistence of two central themes. Our victimizations occur because of the lack of responsibility shown by large industry to consumers and employees, particularly evident in their frequently unscrupulous use of science and technology in the service of profit. The victimizations persist because corporate control of the legislative chambers, administrative agencies, and channels of political communication legitimates the victimization. A selection of particular examples from the corpus of Nader's activities and writings will help to illustrate these points.

The automobile served as a convenient and compelling starting point from which Nader could launch an indictment of the manner in which American society is organized. Critical discussion of this industry was newsworthy (even if Nader did not challenge the very centrality of automobile transportation in American society) because cars not only served as the bellwether of the American economy, but were also intimately tied to our symbolic identities. In magazine articles in the liberal press, in testimony before Congress, and in his *Unsafe at Any Speed,* Nader repeated his charges. He argued that we overemphasized human mistakes in the discussion of auto accidents and failed to note that the consequences of driver error need not have been death if the automobile had been designed with the safety of its occupants in mind. Indeed, most serious injuries were not the result of the initial impact, but were the consequences of the second collision, that of the occupants with part of their own vehicle. He suggested that the devastating consequences of the second collision could, in the majority of cases, be avoided. No overriding reasons could explain why instruments buttons should protrude, or why a driver should be impaled on his steering rod, or why serious injuries should result from the impact of one's head on the dashboard.[4]

Nader accused the auto industry of permitting stylistic concerns to intrude upon the safe design and proper construction of their equipment. Technological innovations that would have improved car safety, he argued, were ignored deliberately and systematically by the automakers. Nader believed that it was justified to consider the auto industry a case of arrested technological development and thus drove a Veblenesque wedge between the activity of business for profit and technological advance. This could be discerned not only in the industry's refusal to implement safety measures but also in its unwillingness to make extensive investigation into other modes of propulsion. Nader quoted with approval an industry critic who noted that it was "not moving up the mainstream of technically based progressive industry groups and that the auto industry had been unprogressive about propulsive systems because of its capital investment in building and servicing the gas gluttonous internal combusion engine."[5] He further believed that this condition was not peculiar to the automakers but was becoming characteristic of the general state of American industry.

By describing what he thought to be the contrary state of affairs in the corporate world, Nader sought to undermine the common belief that large businesses utilize the newest and most efficient technology. He maintained that large firms neither pioneer in the field of social invention nor are readily amenable to changing their regimen through the adoption of existing technological advances. Unlike their predecessors, the ruthless and radical business entrepreneurs, heads of large industrial concerns no longer feverishly implemented marginal improvements in the design and construction of their equipment in order to gain an advantage, however slight and temporary it might be, over their competitors. Instead, firms in the twentieth century reached an innovative watershed after which the transformation of invention into practical application became severely retarded. Nader suggested that this proclivity worked to the detriment of the consumer, for the potential human benefits which might be realized from the utilization of existing technology were infrequently realized in practice.[6]

The exposé of the auto industry, and the paranoid antics of the top industry executives which followed it, gained for Nader the public recognition that he desired. From this base, he detailed other instances of consumer risk and damage to verify his contention that the auto industry should not be perceived as an island of consumer deception in a fundamentally honest business world. Thereafter, he often subsumed the discussion of particular industries under the heading of "business crime." "The harm done to human health and safety by business crime should dispel the distinguishing characteristics of white-collar crime as being the absence of physical threat. Food and drug violations, lavish use of pesticides, defective automobiles, professional malpractice, and building code violations are a much larger hazard to life and limb than crimes of violence on the street."[7] These blanket accusations and his impulse toward systemic indictments angered Nader's more conservative opponents. Despite his refusal to declare a partisan affiliation and his expressed distrust of radical movements, the guardians of American conservatism were not comfortable with Nader's incipient actitivites. Their uneasiness as to his "real" intentions was voiced not long after the publication of *Unsafe at Any Speed.* "What will become of Nader's work is not foreseeable, but that something will come of it is as certain as the rising of tomorrow's sun. That something could be wholly good if kept within the bounds of the safety crusade. But the irritating part of Nader's genius is that it seeks to soar beyond the issue it has successfully raised. What makes Nader a possible menace in addition to being a public benefactor is that he tends toward thinking that corporations are instruments of universal villainy."[8] Still, Nader continued to employ the rhetoric his critics found so distasteful, and it was precisely this "irritating part" which Nader chose to develop by documenting his accusations in a series of case studies.

If the cars we drive provided the most spectacular example of corporate disregard for human safety in everyday life, the food we eat constituted another major source of victimization. With characteristic flair, Nader selected two thoroughly American foods, the hot dog and the hamburger, to be the objects of his attention. He castigated the meat-packing industry for promoting America as a "meat-consuming Valhalla" while through a process of technological adulteration it was transforming diseased and decayed meat into apparently healthy and saleable items. He maintained that the sale of the unsavory "4D" meat was not confined to marginal operators because the profits to be made were sufficient to attract the larger, more prosperous and reputable firms to the practice.[9] His examination of the contents of the hot dog was similarly distressing. He first repeated the familiar refrain that poor sanitation facilities led to the inclusion of insect remains and rodent fragments in resale frankfurters. The more unsettling charge focused on the unscrupulous application of technology, for Nader insisted that the chemical colorings which cosmetically improved the appearance of the meat could also impair the ability of the infant's blood to carry oxygen.[10]

While the auto industry refused to utilize available technological advances, Nader believed that the meat industry was characterized by the consciously deceptive utilization of technology. The connotations of material progress normally associated with scientific understanding and technical application were, according to Nader, entirely illusory here.

> It would be misleading to compare such intrastate operations today with the conditions prevailing at the turn of the century. As far as the impact on human health is concerned, the likelihood is that the current situation is worse. The foul spectacle of packing houses in that earlier period has given way to more tolerable working conditions, but the callous misuse of new technology and processes has enabled today's meat handlers to

> achieve marketing levels beyond the dreams of their
> predecessors avarice. . . . It took some doing to cover up meat
> from a tubercular cow. . . . Now the wonders of chemistry and
> quick freezing techniques provide the cosmetics of camoflaug-
> ing the product and deceiving the eyes, ears, nostrils and taste
> buds of the consumer.[11]

Moreover, the tactics of the meat industry had been adopted by other food providers. Those who might turn to fish to escape the hazards of meat could expect similar problems. Nader noted that the quality "of seafood presented to the housewife in the supermarket each day" was such to make "shopping for seafood akin to playing a slot machine."[12] The reliance on technology to abet deception and victimization served to foreclose for the consumer almost any possibility of making an informed choice because such choice becomes almost impossible when things are not as they appear to be.

Even the clothes we wear constituted another frequently unnoticed source of potential risk. Nader publicized a finding that approximately three thousand lives were literally extinguished each year after a person's garments initially caught fire. He suggested that we could not outfit ourselves or our children in flame retardant material if we so desired because the necessary information concerning the matter was never made available to us by industry representatives. The clothing industry res-ponded to Nader's charges by maintaining that public silence on the issue signified an implicit acceptance of the risk involved each time we donned our clothes. "Consumers don't give a damn about inflammable fabrics. . . . They are much more interested in comfort, wear-life, and lifestyle. . . . It is impossible for the industry to completely insulate a child from the hazards caused by careless and negligent parents or guardians that allow a child to come dangerously close to a source of the flame. This small minority of parents and guardians who fail in this duty should not force the majority of careful and sensible parents to bear the cost of this hardship."[13] Nader argued that the problem was not merely restricted to children; almost anyone was liable to be injured by garment fires—the aged and the infirm being particularly susceptible. Furthermore, the choice between comfort and safety was not the exclusive one the industry represented it to be. We could have both at a negligible price increase if the industry could be persuaded or coerced to show a minimal concern for human safety.[14]

Life at the workplace was a constant source of potential danger in the Nader portrayal, especially for the nonprofessional. More than once he repeated his charge that the "chief source of domestic violence that afflicts American men and women are motor vehicle crashes and occupational hazards and diseases."[15] The occupational malaises ranged from the brown lung disease which workers in cotton mills routinely developed to those caused by overexposure to large doses of X-ray radiation which were acquired by hospital technicians. And, in the most critical industries, Nader charged that safety regulations and preventive measures were either nonexistent or poorly enforced.

Efforts to remedy the incidence of occupational disease were bound to be haphazard and unsystematic because, Nader suggested, any attempt to measure the actual extent of the problem could not be undertaken successfully. "Even data collection reflects the omnipresence of industry. In 1966 less than one half of the states required employees to report all accidents and less than two thirds of the states require employers to keep accident records. . . . Accident and injury reporting in many industries are deliberately aborted in numerous cases. . . . More frequent are make-work activities after injuries and no work such as a worker sitting at a table doing nothing. Data on occupational diseases, such as respiratory and liver ailments from toxic exposures are woefully incomplete."[16] This shortcoming was further complicated by what Nader had earlier mentioned as the tendency of union leaders to use safety demands as a bargaining chip that could be negotiated out of the final contract.[17] The consequence of corporate intransigence and union inaction was that workers contracted occupational diseases and then were unable to receive payments for the medical treatment which could possibly stem the course of decay.

The attitude of the textile industry towards its employees signified a further development in industrial callousness, and once more the complaint focused on the relation between business and science. Here the case was not one of arresting technological development or of utilizing technology as a sophisticated instrument of deception, but one of suppressing basic scientific research. In one particular case, a certain firm endeavored to restrain the dissemination of information in a scientific journal. The company threatened to fire professional staff for scholarly publication of research which concluded that presumed safe levels of certain toxins were in need of significant revision downward. The consequences of this practice, Nader maintained, could have industry-wide repercussions. "Unless each physician, each industrial hygeneist and safety engineer has available to him the research experience of all those who preceded him in his profession, he must duplicate the research in every case, often at the cost of human life."[18] Nader's exposés invariably led to the conclusion that the partnership between business and science is one of convenience in which the former will ignore the demands of the latter if profit margins are threatened.

Recently, Nader has waged campaigns on behalf of public safety against the further development of nuclear power plants. Calling this development a form of "technological suicide," he has proposed that we try instead to discover methods of energy conservation. According to Nader, the risks involved from potential leaks overshadow the presumed benefits which might accrue from the utilization of nuclear power. The use of nuclear power may become, in Nader's mind, the ultimate victimization, one in which the peaceful use of technology necessarily entails warlike consequences for ourselves and for future generations.[19] Nader's opposition to nuclear power is of particular interest because it represents a potential departure from his standard posture toward technology. While his position here is entirely consistent with his campaigns that have focused on consumer safety, this is his first recognition of the destructiveness that is almost inherent in some technologies and of the need to wrest the control of technology from profit-oriented firms. If the technocratic stance taken by public-interest reformers is ever to be altered in the years to come, this realization must surely be further elaborated.

Nader's perspective on the typical function of Washington politics becomes clear when the incidents he has described are kept in mind. Put simply, Washington politics is the arena in which all the aforementioned victimizations receive the congressional and administrative stamp of approval, either through inaction or positive legislation designed for the benefit of large economic concerns. Moreover, the antiquated rules and formal organization of Congress could not serve this purpose better. "Two consequences continually mark the process. First a tradeoff becomes automatic; you scratch my satrap and I'll scratch yours. Second, the problem of control by the lobbying industries is remarkably simplified. . . . The bankers run the Senate Banking Committee, agribusiness runs Agriculture. . . . The federal legislature faithfully reflects the power alignments in society. Power goes to the senior senators who serve powerful interests, while isolation goes to those who merely represent powerless people."[20] It is critical to note that what emerges from the congressional process in the Nader analysis is not merely a set of decisions benefiting the "special interests," but the beginning of a legitimation process in which the public is informed that its wishes have been translated in legislation. Since his appearance as a public figure, Nader has directed his efforts toward both of these problems: he works within the congressional maze to modify some of the decisions that will be reached, and he also strives to provide information to the public that will undermine the self-serving claim of many congressmen to be faithful public servants.

Victimization and Responsibility: The Politics of Self-Defense

If this portrayal of Nader's activities is accurate, I think that we have to admit that his analysis of contemporary life and his version of liberalism musters little support for those who characterize liberals as invariable optimists or naive do-gooders striving to perfect a fallible mankind. Granted, there is a strand of optimism within Nader, for he does believe that organized citizen action can generate beneficial results, but this is certainly distinct from a belief in the perfectibility of mankind or even from adhering to a simple-minded faith that things are getting better. Moreover, we shall see that the sort of activity that Nader endorses is primarily defensive because it is motivated more by a wish to control the practices which diminish the fulfillments offered by the system than by a desire to seek alternative sources of fulfillment. In this sense, Nader's work can be rightly perceived as a method of calling in the warranty on the promises offered by our economic and political institutions.

As a response to the horrors which he has presented so dramatically, Nader proposes that we adopt a posture of political responsibility. A fundamental tenet of his ideology is that the persistent victimizations which reduce the enjoyment of our private pleasures can only be halted by a political praxis which calls those responsible to task. Responsibility must be chosen, for the end result of inaction is complicity in our own victimization. Responsible politics, according to Nader, encompasses a wide range of activities. The principal elements are: (1) the exertion of a countervailing force to the primacy of corporate power in Washington, D.C., (2) the establishment of countervailing forces to the abuses of corporate power within organizations and (3) the development of a local and community-oriented citizen/consumer politics that will be permanently vigilant against corporate abuse.

The initial point of countervailing pressure in the scheme of responsible politics is Nader's own efforts in Washington, D.C., to sever the connection between corporate America and the political establishment. This activity comprised much of Nader's earliest activism as he was perceived as a one-person pressure machine for the public interest. Nader lobbied in Congress, testified before congressional committees, and wrote articles in the liberal press. Nor was Nader above using the procedures of power politics to obtain his goals. When a member of Congress wavered on a piece of legislation of particular importance to Nader, he threatened to denounce him in his hometown press or intimated that he was thinking of organizing a group based in the representative's district to mount an electoral challenge. Throughout all these undertakings, Nader fairly consistently emphasized the regularity of corporate victimization, the hidden methods by which the government has contributed to and legitimized these victimizations, and the necessity to alter both the procedures and the personnel which have been historically connected to this occurrence.

An additional element of the politics of self-defense in Washington has been the establishment of a public-interest "bureaucracy" under Nader's aegis or loosely affiliated with him. This network is supposed to function as a permanent representative of the public interest that can utilize the same tactics that the special interests have honed to perfection. The "bureaucracy" is actually a number of semi-permanent task-oriented projects which seek to influence congressional legislation and administrative proceedings.[21] The members of this entourage were recruited primarily from the legal profession because lawyers supposedly possess the expertise and the language which are the prerequisites to operating successfully in the legislatic atmosphere of Washington politics. Furthermore, given Nader's contention that a primary source of corporate power has been its capacity to legalize the "silent violence" it perpetuates (aided, of course, by the ethics of the legal profession which has condoned furthering these interests), a countervailing organization devoted to the practice of "responsible law" was required. Nader argued that this was especially true in the area of antitrust enforcement where broaching the tenets of free enterprise had been undertaken with impunity and gone basically unchallenged.

Equally important, however, to the long-term stability and success of Nader's projects was the recruitment of politicized scientists and technical experts capable of battling the hired expertise of corporate America with knowledge geared toward public ends. These staff members were people well-versed in the idiom of technology, able to do solid case-study research and capable of presenting their findings in a persuasive manner. The necessity for the recruitment of doctors, scientists, and other technically competent professionals to Nader's cause is directly related to the analysis of victimization. Since the exploitation of consumers involved the "increasing complexity of trying to keep up with the new kinds of swindles that are perpetrated," the exploitation can only be successfully challenged, in Nader's perspective, by a political movement capable of exposing the interests camouflaged by scientific idiom. The composition of Nader's health research group illustrates this attempt to combine scientific and legalistic expertise. The full-time staff is comprised of eight members—of which four are lawyers, three are public health specialists, and one is a physician.[22]

A final element of the Washington operation is its connection with citizens in the localities. The most visible link, of course, is the financial connection in which thousands of Americans contribute to the Public Citizen organization which supports Nader's campaigns. In turn, Nader utilizes the available funds for his efforts at providing more rights for citizens and supporting his various projects. The Public Citizen agenda, in Nader's words, "centers on the fundamental *empowerment* movement. Empowerment means specific rights, remedies and mechanisms accorded people that enable them to defend or assert their interests as consumers, taxpayers and citizens. . . . The idea of empowerment points to a democratic process that needs continual review to determine where excessive or abusive power—by corporations, by government, and by coercive institutions—calls for more corrective powers to the people."[23] A less noticeable but important linkage is the unaffiliated citizen who provides information regarding his or her grievances to Nader who then takes the appropriate steps when a discernible pattern of abuse emerges.

The second principal focus of the politics of self-defense is found in Nader's efforts to spur an increase in on-the-job citizenship. By this he means not what a socialist who advocates workers-control might presume but a mental state of readiness by individuals to "blow the whistle" on illicit practices of their companies. Once again, this is a direct outcome of the victimization theme because the pragmatic rationale for encouraging corporate disloyalty is that the individual worker is the first to be cognizant of the potential abuses. "Most of this country's abuses are secrets known to thousands of insiders, at times right down to the lowest paid worker. A list of Congressional exposures in the poverty, defense, consumer fraud, environmental, job safety and regulatory areas over the past five years would substantiate that observation again and again."[24] Whistle-blowing is consistent with the general tenor of Nader's politics because, when performed correctly, it "has illuminated dark corners of our society, saved lives, prevented injuries and disease, and stopped corruption, economic waste, and material exploitation."[25]

The need for intra-organizational activity is explained by depicting the modern corporation as a feudal governmental structure in which the serfs are systematically desensitized to the practices by which the public interest is undermined. "Today arbitrary treatment of citizens by powerful institutions has assumed a new form, no less insidious than that which prevailed in an earlier time. The "organization" has emerged and spread its invisible chains. Within the structure of the organization, there has taken place an erosion of both human values and the broader value of human beings as the possibility of dissent within the hierarchy has become so restricted that common candor requires uncommon courage."[26] Under these stifling conditions, Nader claims that a sense of allegiance to the public interest has atrophied as citizen silence becomes the accepted and expected mode of behavior.

The final strategy to instigate a successful politics of self-defense—and one Nader has stressed more heavily in recent years—is the development of a politicized society in which citizen/consumers routinely participate. The necessity for the establishment of this complementary form of activity is the recognition that most victimizations occur within twenty-five miles of the home. "Contrary to most popular impressions; the greatest tyranny in the country is not from Washington, it is not from New York, it is the local tyranny. It is the most insistent and most efficient tyranny as far as people living in the locality are concerned . . . , and so, contrary to those bogeys of federalism, its the local community level where the action has to be if we are going to have a more vital community responsible to state and federal governments."[27] A responsible politics must include a greater measure of citizen participation in our political and economic institutions. "The people's loss of the power to govern has deepened as the need for such self-government has risen. Certainly the costs of citizen powerlessness are escalating, if only because people are being affected in more ways by more events out of their control."[28] Without the creation of citizens, Nader believes that his movement is destined for a series of limited victories. "Building a new way of life around citizen action must be the program of the immediate future. The ethos that looks upon citizenship as an avocation or an opportunity must be replaced with a commitment to citizenship as an obligation, a continual receiver of our time, energy and skill."[29] In keeping with this analysis of citizenship as an obligation, Nader advocated mandatory voting in 1973, required that potential summer interns comment on the virtues of this proposal, and has supported the strategy of campus PIRGs (public-interest research groups) to have contributions be deducted automatically from the student fees of every student.

Perhaps the most significant and interesting feature of Nader's progress as an activist is that the level of participation that he has deemed proper and necessary to combat victimization effectively has become increasingly more extensive. While Nader has not challenged the propriety of a for-profit economy, he now appears to believe that the marketplace can only be saved by removing its self-appointed guardians and implementing direct consumer control. In this vein, Nader has recently suggested that the formation of consumer cooperatives "rooted in the community and the neighborhood" is one of his movement's ultimate goals. Although this idea might be said to embody what his opponents have labeled an "anti-capitalist bias," it is probably best interpreted by noting that Nader has simply concluded that consumer justice will remain elusive without consumer control.[30]

The Blinders of Liberalism:
Restricted Politics, Narrow Victimization

The concluding section of this chapter raises objections to Nader's activity which also apply to defensive liberalism as a political stance. My argument claims that his notion of politics is insufficiently broad and that his conception of victimization, while significant, ignores some of the more important victimizations to which we are exposed. An appropriate starting point for comment is Nader's grounding of much of our political activity in the problems we face as consumers of goods and services. Tactically, of course, consumerism appears to be a good set of issues on which reformers can build a constituency. No one likes to breathe polluted air every day, buy a lemon for a car, or pay more for goods in the supermarket solely because one resides in an economically depressed area. Consumer politics makes a visible connection to our daily lives, and this is extremely important because much of contemporary politics fails to do so or succeeds in a very tenuous fashion. Consumerists have convinced people that the barely comprehensible intrigues in Washington result in concrete and real effects on the quality of their material lives. In developing their methods of political action, consumerists have tried to persuade us that enlightened self-interest demands participation, and that by refusing to become engaged, we endorse our continued victimization. In this regard, the politics of self-defense is linked to a politics of fear. People are urged to participate by having the hell scared out of them. But the strategic benefits of this approach are neither long lasting nor conducive to fostering the stated goal of continued popular participation in the decisions which shape our lives.

Nader's approach betokens an implied acceptance of the idea that the most worthwhile activities in human affairs are consumption activities. Politics is the unfortunate business in which we need to be involved if we are to guarantee the continued enjoyment of our consumer benefits. It is that nasty tasting medicine which we gulp and swallow to ward off the germs which could totally debilitate us. A dichotomy is constructed with consumption as a worthwhile pursuit occupying one pole and politics the grimy yet necessary activity the other. This perspective on politics as essentially unpleasant is not at all uncommon and, given the shabbiness of so much of our politics, often quite accurate. Consider the explanation Thomas d'Alesandro offered telling reporters why he would not run for re-election as mayor of the city of Baltimore.

> Every day, I get up, there's a nice limousine waiting for me, the chauffeur opens the door and says 'Good morning, Mr. Mayor.' I get here, come in, everybody is greeting me respectful. I come into this nice office with the big desk. The secretary comes in-'Good morning, Mr. Mayor' and holds out a big silver tray full of shit. 'Would you please eat this Mr. Mayor.' Well, it takes all day: but I finally eat it and go home. And the next morning when I come in, she has a fresh platter of shit for me to eat.'[31]

The commentator on d'Alesandro's unusual withdrawal speech, Garry Wills, can only serve to corroborate this insight. Regarding the vocation of politics, Wills writes: "The real trick of being a politician is to persuade yourself that it is ice cream. Tommy could not meet the test—he kept remembering what he had to eat."[32] Nader's rationale for political activity seems to be in fundamental agreement with the ex-mayor's statement about the unpleasantness of the activity. Unfortunately, because we cannot trust both those who provide consumer goods and those who supposedly represent the public, politics becomes a necessity for everyone.

Let there be no misinterpretation here. The claim is not that politics can ever avoid dealing with grimy topics and other necessary chores which any of us will find distasteful. Nor is it to deny the nobility and integrity which attaches itself to the persons who undertake these chores. I have a friend who is a member of a local board of aldermen. Because water and sewage happen to be political issues in Orange County, North Carolina, he also sits on the county water and sewer authority. On these issues, I gladly authorize him to participate for me. My primary concern is that we get our fair share of water at an equitable rate and that our excrement is disposed of without undue complication. The problem arises, however, when we begin to think that all politics and public life is a duty equivalent to serving on the sewage authority.

Perhaps we need to admit that our current disaffection may also be an outcome of how we have learned to think about politics. If it is unpleasant and unsavory, should we be surprised when those at the top turn out to be machiavellian characters? Hannah Arendt has suggested that it is not so much that power corrupts, but that our recently exposed politicians were corrupt long before they attained their highest office. Now while Arendt's comment may overlook the corrosive effect that power has on those divided souls who contain elements of both good and evil, it does show that our way of thinking about politics, a way adopted by many liberal reformers, becomes a prophecy that is wickedly self-fulfilling. Yet as long as reformers accept this conception and reduction of the political, they will never escape the free-rider dilemma that plagues all liberal efforts to foster political participation and intrigues those who speak about economic theories of democracy.[33] Why should we get involved and get involved permanently, we might ask, if we can rely on Mr. Nader who is so much more skillful and informed to perform these unpleasant activities with our proxies?

We need only look so far as the popular descriptions of Nader to see how true this contention is. What comes immediately to mind are the set of headlines lauding him as the "watchdog" of the public interest or as our "ombudsman" in Washington. But initiatory and participatory democracy needs citizens, not watchdogs or ombudsmen. Focusing on Nader as the representative of a nebulous interest called the public tends to obscure this. Instead, discussion focuses on Nader the personality: is he good or bad? What is he really "up to"? And eminent journalists endorse him for president because he appears to be the one man who has escaped most hints of political taint.

Furthermore, Nader's politics of self-defense implies a sense of certainty about who we are, what we want, and what we should desire that is probably not warranted. Nader simply assumes that our needs and wants as consumers of goods and services should comprise the substance of our political strivings. His call for participation echoes the wisdom that you may not be interested in politics but politics is interested in you, especially your economic self. Nader's delimitation of the political seems to ignore the possibility that participation can serve as an educational contribution to the self-development of individuals, just as it also ignores the intrinisic worth of performing cooperative work with our fellow men and women. Genuine participatory politics that can encourage continued, and not sporadic, forays into the political arena needs to contain a sense of openness, positivity, and sociability which Nader's conception of politics implicitly dismisses. This is not to say that we cannot have political goals worthy of protracted action to be furthered by "agitation and propaganda" or that we should not feel keenly disappointed when important proposals fail to be enacted, but to maintain that sustaining and permanent participation, however, springs from a sense of pride in our collective accomplishments that recognizes the dignity we can achieve and the growth that can be experienced through public deeds. Nader manages to omit these issues from discussion by connecting political action so intimately to our experience as consumers. The consequence is that even the most vigorous expression of contemporary progressive activism is unlikely to generate the enduring commitment to participatory politics which it endorses.

Nader's consumerism is one outgrowth of a conception of politics which encloses the activity within the boundaries of who gets what, when and how. This statement is not intended to belittle the importance of Lasswell's definition. Issues which fall under this rubric constitute vital practical matters and will frame for some time an important segment of our political discourse. We probably could not banish economic issues from our political agenda, and it would be unreasonable to attempt it. John Schaar expressed this point well when he wrote that "accurate social perception is nearly impossible across a huge and uneven social terrain."[34] It is difficult to conceive of an alternative politics which does not also achieve a much greater degree of economic fairness and equality than we presently have. But as citizens and students of politics, we need to encourage and to develop forms of participation which do not always begin and end with a description of whose ox is getting gored. Political disaffection cannot be revitalized by purifying and "massifying" our historical distrust; instead, this task involves the demonstration that politics can possibly carry something other than the shabby connotations with which it is presently saddled.

These reflections also bear on the role that trust and mistrust should play in our political lives. An important part of Nader's work has been his repeated assertion that what he perceives to be a widely held belief in the beneficence and benignity of Washington politics needs to be altered. Events of recent years have undoubtedly aided him in his efforts, but it is also evident that participation does not automatically spring from mistrust. His emphasis on victimization can sometimes lead to the unintended consequence of having people retreat more securely into their privatized shells. Nader is correct to argue that the machinations which occur in Washington cannot be ignored, and mistrust of official rhetoric appears to be a tenable starting point for action. Activists, however, should not stop here or be content with extending the politics of mistrust to more localities. Instead they face the difficult task of working for equity in places where economic goods are allocated, while concurrently striving to build alternative political communities based on trust and competence rather than anxiety and fear.

Nader's insistent efforts to connect political activity to our everyday lives is significant and should be instructive to those activists who formulate their dogmas with little or no reference to the anxieties which pervade the life of most Americans. Nader recognizes, however, only the most explicit instances of victimization and fails to notice the deeper and more insidious victimizations that our society routinely engenders. We could be quite certain that if consumerism achieved its goals tomorrow, genuine and significant victimizations would not cease to plague us. A mundane example can be used to illustrate this. Consumer advocates have been concerned for some time with the safety of sleeping pills. They discovered many brands to be insufficiently pretested and potential dangers to be frequently mislabeled and sometimes even unlabeled. To remedy these defects consumerists have labored to persuade government officials and federal agencies to exert stricter control over the manufacture and distribution of sleeping pills. These are legitimate concerns, and it would take an unusually mean-spirited person to argue that lobbying which might ensure the safety of sleeping pills should not be undertaken. None of these efforts, however, addresses the question of why we spend millions of dollars to go to sleep in the evening. With the aid of a few politicized scientists, it is easy to politicize the former concern —though not equally simple to *win* as the multiple struggles of the consumerists have indicated. As of now, we have no real idea of how to go about politicizing the latter concern. Those who currently appeal to our fears do so more for their personal electoral advantage than from any desire to aid us in describing and overcoming the actual sources of our collective anxieties.

We need to become more conscious than Nader of the victimizations which occur as a result of linking status and self-worth to the pursuit of consumer goods. It is curious that an ascetic such as Nader has never really politicized the issue of life-style but has instead concentrated on making the pursuit of consumer goods more worthwhile. But his remedies of competition, regulation, a purified technology, and increased citizen participation are not, by themselves, conducive to reducing the anxiety which the race produces. One need only think of Marx's description of Adam Smith's frenetic world to realize this. Nader's emphasis on collective participation is important and may be a significant component of an improved polity that is not dependent on the values of a high consumption society. This participation, however, has to be refashioned in a more positive manner than it is in his defensive liberalism.

Furthermore, the problems involved in the utilization of technology are even more complex than Nader indicates. He correctly describes the need to improve car safety and the need to expose and prohibit the practices of those who employ technological means to disguise the actual quality of their merchandise. Who would question that we need scientists attuned to the delicate political implications of their work and technicians who are not hesitant to speak out when scientific processes are used to deceive the consumer in the supermarket? But the problems of technology are embedded so deep that they will only be partially addressed by the development of a scientific bureaucracy with a "human face." We have to speak, as was shown in Chapter Two, not only about using technology more efficiently and less destructively, but also about criticizing technology and limiting its sphere of influence. Most importantly, we have to work to ensure that matters are not described to be technical and apolitical when these are really issues which should be subject to collective, moral, and prudential decisions.

These are not only Nader's problems. As students of politics, we often find ourselves in a similar quandary. Our methodologies can be extremely accurate in describing who got what, when, and how; but these are much less accurate in describing and evaluating the pattern of human relationships that is involved in the provision of goods and services. Students of politics need to draw a clearer picture of the links which connect these aspects of our everyday life to our social and political mores. It is important that we understand and articulate all the fears, anxieties, and victimizations which are interwoven together with the purported benefits of market society that undergird so much of liberal theory and confront and plague us as liberal people. It is especially important to those interested in progressive political change because social movements and attempted political alterations can only succeed to the extent that these movements are capable of describing, confronting, publicizing, and eventually transcending these fears.

Chapter 4

The Consumer in American Politics

Political activists must have certain virtues; but theoretical rigor and consistency are hardly at the top of the list. We no doubt hesitate to endorse the politics of someone whose ideas are hopelessly muddled, but we are not usually distraught at the prospect of supporting a political figure who does not, as a matter of course, ruthlessly follow his ideas to their logical conclusion. Rigor and consistency are not normally the preeminent virtues in political life: indeed, the obligations of an activist frequently preclude him from obtaining the necessary time and requisite distance from the cause which make these intellectual accomplishments possible. As concerned citizens, we are typically undismayed that public actors do not take time off for extensive reflection. We would rather count on public figures to follow their humane intuitions than to lose their efforts while they retreat to libraries for intellectual sustenance. If a political reformer is to be evaluated primarily according to the criteria of rigor and consistency, a justification for this uncustomary procedure is necessary.

Nader is surely a cut above the average progressive reformer in regard to rigor and consistency. But although he has not been especially reflective concerning the nature of his entire enterprise, he has managed to explain cogently the reasons underlying many of his undertakings. The intellectual caliber of his analyses is unusually high in comparison to those of others on the contemporary political scene. His writings have appeared in liberal intellectual weeklies and respected law journals. Despite this facility of expression, it would still seem inappropriate to evaluate him according to the internal consistency of writings and actions. He is first and foremost an activist, and therefore he has a *prima facie* claim to be judged as other political figures. This includes on empathetic recognition of the consequences that practical engagement invariably generates—that is, the acceptance of half loaves, the occasional compromise with principle, and the inconsistencies manifested in intuitive responses.

There are times, however, when we have a right and also a need to demand more from our progressive reformers than an ingenious manipulation of existing procedures and institutions for our benefit. This is true even if these activities are performed with an unquestionable sense of moral commitment. The present occasion is one in which there is a grave need to do more than rummage cleverly within the established ideological confines. We are required to sit down and clarify the concerns, goals, and methods of our common life. In the past few decades, most of our ameliorative proposals have implied that reforms could be discovered, legislated, and implemented without permanently threatening the material perquisites of the wealthy.

For example, we could have a war on poverty without assaulting the bastions of privilege. We could have law and order while continuing to articulate an ideology of feckless individualism, and we could have a livable environment without adjusting our prodigal habits. No longer can these assumptions be taken for granted. The inconsistency at the core of the belief that threatening social problems can be resolved without modifying the foundations of a consumer society has become increasingly obtrusive. It is not clear, however, that our liberal reformers have acknowledged this.

The preceding two chapters have explained the purpose and the ideology animating Nader's progressive reformism. His repeated demonstrations that the system does not function as benignly as its defenders claim have lent genuine significance to his actions. But I have also contended that his politics tend to obscure the deeper victimizations we experience as a result of our attachment to consumer goods and our quest to acquire them. The intent of this chapter is to demonstrate that these objections to Nader's emphases are not capricious or eccentric but eminently practical.

The initial section introduces the contradictions that develop within Nader's liberal reformism when he tries to convince us that consumerism can legitimately be considered harmonious with the demands of environmental reasonableness. The body of the chapter distinguishes the priority of consumer satisfaction from the asserted imperatives of ecological concern. I argue that Nader has been correct to link political action with a conception of the public interest, but maintain that his emphasis on consumer satisfaction mitigates his capacity to do so convincingly. Political ecologists are shown to be better attuned than Nader to the problems caused by the escalation of consumer wants, but are criticized for exhibiting greater interest in simply restraining these wants than in altering the social and economic conditions which give rise to these drives. The conclusion offers some tentative recommendations that liberal reformers who have been concerned with consumer victimizations might follow so that their actions could reflect a greater sensitivity to conditions of limited resources than is presently the case.

Self-Interest and Scarcity:
Nader's Contradiction

Nader's legislative influence, though not as pervasive as he thinks appropriate, has been significant in areas other than the establishment of fair laws for the retail consumer. Environmental regulation has been a policy field of especial importance to Nader and other public-interest reformers. Groups under his supervision or loosely affiliated with him have worked aggressively and energetically for reduction of environmental pollution at the workplace, for stricter controls on automobile emissions, for prevention of nuclear power plant construction, and for application of criminal sanctions to conscious defilers of the environment. To be sure, ecological politics has also enlisted the hearty support of people other than Naderites; it could not be accurately described as a Nader "citizens' crusade." Yet much of the direct political activity on this front has been performed under Nader's aegis, and his efforts at lobbying, organization building, and information dissemination have contributed to the limited success which has been garnered. Nader and other public-interest reformers have depicted their environmentalist concerns as consistent with their consumerist proposals; indeed, ecological politics is often considered a complementary element of the movement.

This natural association between consumerism and environmentalism is evoked by describing the hazardous ecological effects of "passive consumption." Nader describes what he considers the decrease experienced in the quality of our lives because of the paucity of constraints on the industrial disposal of wastes. He argues that because of corporate malfeasance, we drink contaminated water, breathe excessively polluted air, and labor in unhealthy environments.[1] Since stricter governmental regulation is frequently thought to be an appropriate remedy in these matters, Nader has utilized tactics similar to those he has employed on behalf of retail consumers to submit the private sector to the requisite controls. Nader's subsumption of environmentalism under the mantle of consumerism is not, however, an entirely acceptable conceptual formulation. Consumerism and environmentalism can only be tactically united to form the "public interest" when we are examining the lowest common denominator of both movements. It is plausible to assume that we cannot enjoy consumer satisfactions broadly defined or have an environmentally viable society without relatively clean air and uncontaminated water.[2] But Nader has not addressed the accusation made by "strict environmentalists" that the spiraling creation of consumer wants in a capitalist society is environmentally destructive. His differentiation between active and passive consumption has not included an accounting of the ill effects that routinely pursuing the former may have on the latter.

Consumerism and environmentalism which Nader has ingeniously united in a linkage of convenience are theoretically, and eventually politically, incompatible. This incompatibility is best discerned in the attitudes regarding private consumption behavior which premise the two movements. A principal aim of consumerism is to regulate the pernicious conduct of corporate enterprise and increase our satisfaction by acquiring the goods that our economic system makes available. A society populated by individuals striving to obtain as many of these products as they possibly can is taken as the context in which political action will occur and not as a condition which is itself problematic. Economic self-interest, so long as it is pursued safely and tempered by a commitment to political involvement, is considered a suitable motivation for both personal and political action. Liberal reformers have infrequently challenged this assumption or publicly advocated its modification. Nader has rarely commented on the inner destructiveness that the desire to acquire consumer goods may engender, and he has paid scant attention to the possible resource limits that the progressive escalation of these drives may push us. His indictment of the automobile industry discussed in Chapter Three is a case in point. Despite the stir which his accusations begat, Nader refrained, both then and now, from advancing additional criticism of the mores which made our identities partially dependent on the cars we drove and of the transportation policies which ultimately fueled our energy anxieties by creating the necessity of individual car ownership.

Strict environmentalists are more outspoken in these matters and aver that our habitual means of obtaining satisfaction are ecologically destructive and possibly survival threatening. They believe that the objective fact of resource scarcity necessitates a style of social and political organization antithetical to arrangements which permit economic self-interest to operate unhampered and foster the proliferation of consumer wants. Political ecologists find an unsettling and perhaps moral excessiveness in our devotion to products. One of their primary counsels equates the practice of a moral life with restraint in the consumption of goods. E.F. Schumacher has expressed this sentiment. "The optimal pattern of consumption, producing a high rate of human satisfaction by means of a relatively low rate of consumption, allows people to live without great pressures and strains and to fulfill the primary injuction of Buddhist teaching: 'Cease to do evil, try to do good.' ''[3]

This moral enjoinder has been linked by political ecologists to what they consider a practical necessity in their forecasts about our decreasing capacity to sustain the prodigality of a growth economy. At times, they suggest that we learn to do more with less. On other occasions, they maintain that we can keep our present standard of living intact by reducing wasteful consumption. But in no instance do they hold that we can continue to follow a politics of rising expectations on a societal scale. Indeed, in the estimation of some scholars, the objective reality of scarcity will be accompanied by major alterations in the actual possibilities for consumption. Robert Heilbroner's speculations in his *An Inquiry into the Human Prospect* well illustrate this position. "Thus the difficulty of managing a socially acceptable distribution of income in capitalist nations is that it will have to contend with a decline in the per capita output of material goods. The problem is therefore not merely calling a halt to the increasing production of cars, dishwashers and homes, but of distributing a shrinking production of cars, dishwashers and homes."[4] If Schumacher's statement is simply an injunction that we lead more ascetic lives, Heilbroner's analysis is a prophecy regarding our eventual submission to an environmental imperative. His belief is that America's devotion to the consumer culture will be altered, if not by deliberate choice, then certainly from the pressure of circumstantial necessity.

Those who speak of an environmental imperative, as we shall see in greater detail below, believe that a significant disparity exists between political action grounded in economic self-interest and the foundations of a politics that can effectively ward off ecological threats. Political ecologists would admit that most of us desire the particular elements of an ecologically sound world but simultaneously tell us that our self-interested economic wishes routinely conflict with the exigencies of an adequate environmental policy. Nader's strategic ingenuity has to be unmasked and his inconsistency exposed not to demonstrate that a specific reformer has been slipshod in his logic but to show that his tactical savvy is insufficient for resolving the fundamental questions with which we are faced. In this respect, Nader can be evaluated as an activist who has undeniably furthered the cause of environmental reasonableness but who has also primarily identified himself with a movement containing tendencies which obstruct the implementation of necessary ecological measures. Although effective in placing some environmental issues on the legislative agenda, Nader obscures the magnitude of the personal and political alterations that may have to be chosen.[5]

But what if, it might be objected, the emphases and pessimistic scenarios of these environmentalists are exaggerated and, in the end, the technological optimists prove to have divined the true outcome? If scientific advances and improved technology do manage to solve the dilemmas of feeding an expanding population, husbanding a sufficient supply of resources, and combating pollution troubles, has the time spent here discussing Nader's inconsistency been wasted? I happen to think not. In the highly improbable event that political ecologists are discovered to have been grossly mistaken in their specific predictions, they still have influenced the potential for an improvement of our political discourse in a salutary manner. Most importantly, they have provided a practical and tangible context in which to place the fundamental inadequacies of conventional liberal politics. Writers have criticized for more than a decade the consumer model of man found at the core of American politics. But they have been unable to connect their analyses attesting to the desirability of altering our economic and psychological foundations with the experiential factors that might mandate these changes. Ecological anxiety, even if somewhat overstated, has opened the possibility that the consumer model of man can be seriously challenged in a practical manner. The dialogue which should now proceed is a fitting example of that in which John Gunnell urged us to engage when he wrote that the function of political studies is to find a home for man in the world.

The Priority of Consumer Satisfaction

Nader's politics, as already described, have not questioned the reasonableness of a society in which a high "standard of living" refers to the availability of a complete array of consumer satisfactions. This section begins by demonstrating that Nader's attempt to define his activities as a genuine "public-interest" movement is unsuccessful because of the difficulties of grounding a common good in our preferences as consumers. It next suggests that the efforts we put forth to obtain freedom and autonomy through the acquisition of consumer goods can be understood to signify, in part, a reaction to the restricted alternatives of our public world. The purchased autonomy of private life is largely illusory, however, because in obtaining it we concurrently acquiesce to and reinforce the corporate definitions of proper behavior. Nader, critical of corporate excesses, aware that we need to speak of a common good, yet still wedded to the values of commercial society, is metaphorically characterized as our "last liberal."

A vast literature in the disciplines of economics, political science, and political philosophy is relevant to the claims about to be presented. Two significant notions found throughout this body of scholarship will be mentioned briefly in order to lay the groundwork for the following argument about Nader. The first idea distinguishes between the expressed preference of an individual, on the one hand, and, on the other, those actions which actually further his welfare. Although these may often coincide, an individual or a collectivity can state and act upon a preference severely detrimental to his/its welfare. For example, imperfect information may lead consumers to buy goods which undermine their well-being. Think of the thousands of shoppers who have purchased meats unaware of the possible connection between red-dye number two and their susceptibility to cancer. Furthermore, even if we presume that a perfect market condition in respect to information does exist, an individual may select an option of which the short-term benefits are positively harmful to his ultimate welfare. Smokers who have witnessed the effects of emphysema among their relatives may still persist in their two-pack-a-day habit.

A second consideration of relevance to the discussion of Nader is the problematic nature of the public-interest concept when it is utilized in conjunction with an intellectual perspective or political movement of which the underlying premise is to maximize individual consumer preferences. Political scientists and economists have entered into a recurring dialogue about whether it is actually possible to order and aggregate preferences so that the results will reflect the desires of the majority. My analysis of Nader's utilization of the public-interest concept will not focus on the mathematical conundrums with which he is faced, but will instead point to the theoretical and ideological inadequacy of a reformist liberalism that assays to speak of a public good in the vocabulary of consumer preferences.[6]

The notion of consumer satisfaction, in its embryonic form, bears a negative connotation. In this sense, it has more to do with our fears and anxieties than it does with our positive wants and desires. This negative connotation signifies freedom from anxiety while we perform our role within the system. According to Nader, this means not being subjected to unnecessary victimizations while we go about our daily tasks. It implies eating nutritious food, traveling in relative safety to and from the job and working in a healthy environment. It is the legacy of that part of liberalism which enjoins us to avoid pain. Nader's political campaigns typically emphasize these minimal or defensive ingredients of consumer satisfaction. He thus becomes involved with trying to set and implement rigorous standards for automobile accident performance, with attempting to remove dangerous or insufficiently tested drugs from the marketplace and with antinuclear lobbying.

To build a political movement by appealing to our preferences qua consumers, however, denotes more than a wish that we can buy our products with confidence, drive our cars safely, and take medicines that will not instigate a cure worse than the original malaise. I think a consumerist politics implies—and it is Nader's reticence on the matter which I believe validates this statement—that our strivings and efforts should be directed toward acquiring more of these satisfactions. The objection might be raised that we should be hesitant to draw this far-reaching implication because Nader has never voiced explicit testimony to this effect. But even if my claim was reduced to say that Nader's reformism has adopted, with the exception of a safety qualification, the position that "something is in a person's interest if it increases his opportunities to get what he wants . . . whatever that may be," the problems which follow will not be significantly diminished.[7] Whether Nader's appeals to consumers actually foster the multiplication of consumer wants or are simply an affirmation that most consumer preferences constitute legitimate political interests, a set of insoluble dilemmas arise when he equates his actions with serving the public good.

The first shortcoming, as mentioned above, is that preferences may have nothing to do with welfare and since political action is inherently concerned with what "ought to be," it should not and cannot justifiably ignore the demand that politics further the general good. By limiting his conception of welfare essentially to safe consumption, Nader's capacity to speak of the commonweal is also circumscribed. If there are resource limits on consumption and if consumer societies necessarily generate a surplus of internal anxiety, it seems unbecoming for political reformers who purport to work in the public-interest to endorse actions which may result in a headlong rush to personal and collective oblivion. A second failing is that the consumerist rationale does not distinguish those interests which deserve to be protected from those which do not. Furthermore, it does not assign priorities about whose interests deserve immediate attention and whose do not. The lack of discernment in regard to the relative significance of interests has resulted in some embarrassing incidents for Nader and his followers. On more than one occasion, consumer groups have spent an inordinate percentage of their time in the service of the decidedly affluent whose complaints might have been resolved in other channels, leaving the activists to focus their efforts on more important matters elsewhere.

Nader's difficulty in putting the public-interest concept into operation has not gone unnoticed by all his supporters. Although he and his followers usually appraise their reformism to be that of service to the public weal and although this description has served both as a rhetorical device and as a sincere estimation on the activists' part of their sympathies and intentions, a few of his more reflective aides have expressed uneasiness with Nader's public-interest standard. One who worked on his Congress Watch project was bedeviled by what he considered the elusiveness of the concept.

> How could we tell if this particular bill was or wasn't in the public interest? . . . From my vantage point as a profile writer . . . the project had a deeper flaw; the vacuousness of the public-interest standard for evaluating the work of a Congressman. . . . Was it for or against the public interest to support right to work laws? or tax incentives for industrial investment? and what of fundamental conflicts of economic interest between consumers, for example, who want inexpensive bread and farmers who want large incomes? Where does the public interest fall and who is to determine it? If Nader has a method for evaluating these political views, he did not convey it to his Raiders.[8]

Another ex-Raider felt that since such questions were normally resolved by an assertion on Nader's part as to what constituted the public interest, Nader's reformism contained an unacknowledged dangerous element.

> For Nader, as for Rousseau, virtue consists in a passion for the public interest and the wisdom to apprehend it. And it is in the central notion of a public interest that both Nader and Rousseau manifest their most dangerous tendencies. Nader, keenly aware of the decidedly illiberal implications of apriori notions of the public interest, claims the concept is a processual one, referring not to the substance of particular policy decisions but rather to the conditions and procedures under which the decision is arrived at. Nonetheless, his promiscuous use of the phrase and its diabolical opposite, the 'special' interests, raises moral questions with which Nader has never seriously grappled.[9]

While both of these criticisms identify troublesome elements of Nader's politics (with due apologies to Rousseau for the gratuitous reference), neither really penetrates to the root of Nader's failure to speak convincingly of his public-interest standard.

The elusiveness of the public-interest criterion which bothered the profile writer on the Congress Watch project is best explained not by claiming that Nader has absolutely no standards, but by realizing that a consumerist perspective renders impossible the formulation of consistent standards. If one desire (as long as it can be satisfied relatively safely) is as good as another, we cannot really differentiate between a consumer preference that is worthy and one that is unworthy. Furthermore, since Nader's reformism has ignored the thorny questions of political economy by focusing on consumerist matters, he does not have a ready answer to queries which originate outside his definition of political reality. Matters such as tax incentives for industrial investment require that political actors be willing to address the basic role of the private sector in an industrialized nation and perhaps explicitly defend a perspective on the American corporate economy that is typically described as radical.

The aide who commented on the potential danger of Nader's movement objected to Nader's propensity to define the public-interest in a substantive manner prior to ascertaining majority preference through the mechanics of procedural democracy. Less sympathetic critics who have also been disturbed by this tendency have labeled Nader a closet elitist who, by deciding that governmental action should prohibit the consumption of certain harmful products, arrogates to himself decisions that should be made in the free marketplace. The charge of paternalism leveled at Nader is true to the extent that he believes consumption should be safe and routinized, not risky and completely free. This does, of course, restrict the unfettered operation of the market. Moreover, Nader has at times disregarded the processual component that will need to be included in any valid approximation of the public interest and acted as if consumers need to be protected regardless of their expressed wishes.

Yet to point to Nader as a dangerous elitist, who interferes with our liberties by shamelessly telling us what to do, can turn our attention from a more significant weakness. The claim surely exaggerates. Nader accepts the principles of a consumer society, but only asks that safety be taken into account while we consume. More importantly, the inadequacy of his public-interest criterion is not only found in an improper balance of procedural and substantive components, but in the realization that Nader's "public" is exceedingly scrawny. The common bond which unites the members of his public is the experience of being someone's unwitting prey. Yet if we are to create a politics that speaks meaningfully of a *common interest,* we cannot also believe that we only become citizens to further our individual consumer interests. I think that a fundamental element (leaving aside the important questions regarding the balance of procedural and substantive components) of a politics that can be said to work today for the public good is a capacity to moderate the force of our consumer impulses in order to discuss our collective direction and decide on the most equitable manner of sharing our burdens. Nader understands our need to speak in terms of a common good but cannot do so persuasively while frequently limiting the content to consumer appetites.[10]

The belief that the furtherance of consumer preferences constitutes the common interest represents, in part, an accommodation and resignation to the impoverishment of public life in contemporary society. By permitting us to obtain the pleasure not to be gained in the public world as we have found and created it, consumer acquisitions purportedly compensate for the lonely, tension-filled encounters that mar our social experiences. Consider, in this respect, the portrait of anxiety that the sociologist Erving Goffman has sketched in his descriptions of our "relations in public." In Goffman's depiction, our public life has become a series of maneuvers designed to retain "normal appearances" in a world in which few are trusted and in which every stranger is a threat to violate our personal space and perhaps our physical integrity.[11] In this context, consumer satisfactions promise enjoyment free from domination and free, if we wish, from excessive risk-taking. They promise peace and leisure away from the grind, the bustle, and the hustlers of the everyday world.

The choices that men and women make as consumers become their rewards for tolerating the unpleasantness of the nine-to-five world. In fact, many people do try to utilize their consumer purchases to restore a degree of sociability to their lives, a sociability that would in other eras be associated with the public realm. A relatively affluent homeowner, dismayed by the facilities in his community, may sincerely believe that the pool he installs in his backyard is a neighborhood service—a place where the adults can gather to converse while the children splash and dunk. A similar motivation might spur a young blue-collar worker to purchase a color television. He may relish the camaraderie to be had when his friends visit to watch a popular sporting event much more than he appreciates the aesthetic pleasures which viewing the richness of the colors affords him. Thus to be victimized in our cars bespeaks an excessive cruelty, for these moments away from the drudgery of work and the threat of others on the streets are the prizes for which we have labored. The anger that we see well up in a consumer who has been "ripped off" is not merely the consequence of his knowing that one of his preferences has been denied but is an intuitive reaction to someone mocking his identity by violating the implicit social compact.

Forsaking the effort to alter the public world by alternatively striving to acquire the consumer satisfactions available in advanced capitalist society is, in the final tally, an expensive life-strategy. On first examination, the desire to lead the comfortable existence that these goods provide appears to be a reasonable, if not a particularly noble, ambition. Neither the workplace nor life on the streets will be significantly improved by the efforts of a single individual. Furthermore, who wants to be dissatisfied —especially when this is taken in Nader's sense to mean continual manipulation and victimization at the hands of others? Yet the response to this is not so clear-cut if we also ask what sort of persons do we become and what kind of society do we create by readily acceding to such limited conceptions of human freedom? Or, as the younger Mill posed the issue, what happens to us when we permit our identities to be encased within the available satisfactions?

The persistent nagging of this question led to Mill's effort to distance himself from the Benthamites without discarding the utilitarian frame-work. Mill spoke as if he had devised a method for transcending the Benthamite calculus in which push-pin was as good as poetry. His standard which allowed intellectuals to arbitrate disputes about the relative quality of pleasures, however, was not persuasive. Consumerists, unwilling to offer such bold testimony to their capabilities, assay to escape from Mill's bind by means of a tactical refusal to address the issue. Simon Lazarus' remarks about Nader in *The Genteel Populists* puts this gingerliness in its most favorable light.

> Some new populist spokesmen have shown considerable sensi-
> tivity to the conflict between their actual preferences and their
> middle or working class espoused interests. Ralph Nader in
> particular tries to avoid offending these constituencies. Al-
> though he frequently attacks corporate advertising, he avoids,
> at least for the most part, Galbraith's bombast about corpo-
> rate manipulation of societal values. His target is deception,
> something all people can unite to oppose.[12]

But one cannot help but wonder how much of a blessing Nader's reluctance to join this chorus really is for his constituency. If we believe that the "freedom" to be obtained by the purchase of consumer satisfactions is actually undermined by the dependency that ensues after we make this commitment, how thankful should we be that our reformers do not confront the matter? Galbraith's "bombast," and that of many others who propound similar beliefs, is intended to educate us about the duplicity inherent in consumer societies. Individuals are promised that their tensions might be relieved through the acquisition of goods, yet the real sources and causes of their tensions remain as before. Indeed, the perpetual creation of new products and the marketing tactics used to convince us of their necessity frequently lead to the development of new tensions, new anxieties.[13]

Curiously, Nader's life-style and many of his ecological beliefs exhibit a singular disregard for much of what his movement does not criticize publicly. He was once asked by an interviewer if he did not think that consumer societies were a contemporary analogue of Roman decadence. Nader replied that he felt the interviewer might be correct, for he himself did believe that we engaged in too many activities actually destructive to our well-being and spent inordinate time satisfying desires superfluous to the construction of a rewarding life. More important than his actual feelings, however, has been Nader's unwillingness to politicize these intimations and challenge the system which encourages this decadence. He is ultimately trapped in the position of leading a political movement which has an underlying rationale contradictory to a body of his personal beliefs. An argument could be made that Nader has politicized his beliefs through personal example, yet this is not convincing because Nader's example is so eccentric that it is impossible to conceive of anyone but him following that life-style. He has depicted our everyday lives in a mode distinct from that of the system's apologists but has remained unable to criticize its presentation of worthwhile aims.

In one of the most powerful analyses of American politics written in the last decade, Garry Wills argued in *Nixon Agonistes* that Richard Nixon could be appropriately described as the last authentic classical liberal in America.[14] Wills suggested that Nixon's belief in the efficacy and worth of the market was evident in his general disdain for the New Deal and his commitment to dismantle the administrative and regulatory edifice of Franklin Roosevelt. Wills portrayed Nixon's devotion to market values as an internal demon which led him to loathe rest and drove him throughout his life to compete relentlessly only to experience the "loneliness of the long-distance runner." Wills description of Nixon and the citizenry that elected him was undeniably chilling, but I think that the defensive liberal Nader can be metaphorically characterized as our "last liberal" in a more compelling sense. Nader is such a more complex liberal, one with greater insight into the turnings of a liberal-capitalist nation, attuned to its flaws but still firmly bound to it and unable to escape its strictures. Nader is a more insightful liberal because he realizes that the progress and expansion of capitalism requires the government to assume a more interventionist stance than if it operated according to strict principles of laissez-faire. Nader realizes the danger of monopoly capital and would never consider uttering Nixon's "I'm not against bigness per se" when informed of possible antitrust action against ITT and requested to advise a course of action.

Nader also realizes what can happen to individuals who are so thoroughly driven within a democratic-capitalist society. He understands that scientists who work for acquisitive industries may be encouraged to falsify reports about the potential toxicity of their company's products if they want to keep their jobs and further their career opportunities. He understands that presumably decent individuals will manufacture and sell defective merchandise and that meat packers interested in profits may utilize chemical adulterants to pass off decayed meat as if it was fresh. He understands that some politicians might subvert the wishes of their constituents if presented with an opportunity to expand their financial holdings, and he understands why a politician with an untouchable margin in the polls might still be driven to smear a potential opponent. Despite the plethora of significant problems that he recognizes, Nader does not formulate a source of valuation external to the system that he labors to alter. Instead he gives us better competition, stricter regulation, more satisfaction.

The Ecological Summons

While Nader's reformism has not questioned the assumption that our interests qua consumers usually approximate the public interest, a similar reticence is not displayed in works of political ecology. The scholarly writing on environmental politics is not yet characterized by widespread agreement on the appropriate political response so that it would be incorrect to construe the statements below to be the definitive principles of a coherent field called political ecology. Although every environmentalist stresses the necessity of building an ecologically viable society, a general consensus does not exist on the particular strategies and tactics most conducive to achieving this goal. In this section and in Chapter Six, I will be speaking of a highly visible group of political ecologists whose widely publicized opinions have recently gained a measure of popular and scholarly currency. These writers contend that the predictions of impending ecological catastrophe are, in the main, accurate and that immediate alterations of our social and political institutions must be coupled with changes in our personal habits, especially those of breeding and consuming, to insure the continued survival of mankind. The course of their argument beginning with a description of societal excesses and terminating with a call for a new Leviathan is briefly outlined in the next few pages.[15]

The argument of these writers is initiated by an assertion that the normal functioning of our social and political institutions is ecologically hazardous. "Our problem is not so much that our institutions no longer work the way they should—they work only too well even now in permitting the ruthless exploitation of the environment—but the assumptions about the carrying capacities of the commons are no longer true."[16] These writers share Nader's critical perspective on American commercialism but for different reasons. Most pointedly, they contend that the growth economy, dependent on an infinitely renewable supply of resources, is organized on premises not applicable to the contemporary condition. If Nader is demanding that corporate enterprise improve the delivery record on its promises, ecologists suggest that such an improvement is of uncertain benefit because the wasteful utilization of resources and the creation of superfluous needs will persist. According to this interpretation of our ecological needs, major restrictions still must be placed on the traditional liberties of commercial enterprise.

Our political institutions are not currently up to the task because at present these also contribute to the exacerbation of ecological problems. As in Nader's analysis, the process is depicted as one rigged to give disproportionate influence to special interests pushing private concerns. "The great mass of people, who will be indirectly affected and whose personal stake in the outcome is likely to be negligible, have very little incentive to organize in defense of their interests. . . . After all the right decision may be worth $10 million dollars to General Motors while costing each individual a few pennies. Thus those who try to stand up to special interests on environmental issues, find themselves up against superior resources all along the board."[17] Furthermore, almost all public policy makers endorse the anachronistic wisdom of the corporate economy by assuming that a commitment to growth will have to be maintained. Legislators demand an increase in porkbarrel projects, presidents seek to maintain business confidence at all costs, and even reformers place their advocacy for the impoverished within the context of the growth economy.

What makes the immediate rectification of these practices even more unlikely is that the citizenry has fully internalized the conventional goals of political economy. In Ophul's words again: "People want jobs, economic opportunities and a growing economy. Indeed, to the extent that the system has had a guiding policy at all, it has been precisely to satisfy the rising expectations of its citizens. . . . The outcome of the process of

American politics faithfully reflects the will of the people and their desire for economic growth."[18] The obstacles that our habits pose in any effort to meet environmental challenges successfully is most clearly revealed in the popular equation of well-being with expanded consumption. "Our welfare [presently] depends on rapid consumption and more consumers—this is fatal—but [should depend] on the extent we can wring the maximum richness and amenity for a reasonable population from minimum resources."[19] Thus ecologists contend that an adequate response to ecological threats must furnish the means to restrain the prodigal habits of the citizenry as well as altering the direction of our political affairs.

According to this analysis, the environmental imperative calls for a revamped authoritarian government in which purposeful decisions can be made away from the pull and tug of interest-group skirmishes. "If scarcity is not dead, if it is in fact with us in much more intense form than ever before in human history, how can we avoid reaching the conclusion that Leviathan is inevitable. Given current levels of population and technology, I do not believe that we can."[20] The decisions of this government will, of course, not only regulate corporate excesses but will also deny the impulses of the population's consumer appetites. "People must be restrained and the only question is how to go about choosing the necessary ends . . ., because even if we avoid the tragedy of the commons, it will only be by recourse to the tragic necessity of Leviathan."[21] The politics of survival will not tolerate either the anarchy of corporate economic liberty or the childish hedonism of an egoistic citizenry.

The tactical agreements that Nader and these political ecologists might reach on specific legislative matters dissolve when the depths of their respective visions is plumbed. Most of Nader's goals have been fairly immediate, easily comprehensible, and usually capable of being smoothly translated into legislative packages within the existing political arena. Campaigns for mandatory airbags in automobiles, better pretesting of pharmaceuticals, and the establishment of a Consumer Protection Agency are proposals which existing political institutions can handle with a high degree of facility. The goals and proposals of political ecology do not exhibit this smooth fit into our conventional political channels. In a very real sense, these constitute what Benjamin De Mot has called an ecological summons to change your life. These goals can only be successfully realized by a political praxis which opens possibilities previously thought to be unrealistic.

Imagine, in this respect, a conversation that a consumerist and political ecologist might have with a factory worker who drives an air-conditioned

Chevrolet Impala with a 427 cubic inch engine. The consumerist would center his queries on the performance of the car. He might want to discover if any injuries occurred because of faulty internal design when the car was involved in a minor accident, and he might be interested in hearing about the quality of service in the dealership. "Was the warranty work performed promptly and correctly?" The ecologist would less likely by interested in the performance of the car and more prone to see the occasion as one to test his persuasive capacities. He might attempt to convince the owner that it would be in the long-term interest of anyone to trade in the Impala for a compact model. Failing here, the ecologist might resort to the self-interest argument, suggesting that the sacrifice is in the owner's best interest, especially if he includes in this the well-being of his progeny. "Don't you want to leave some of the good things in life for your sons and daughters?" Failing all, our ecologist might abruptly terminate the conversation by remarking that he hopes the price of gas doubles in the next year.

It should be recognized, however, that the restraints deemed necessary by these political ecologists are, in one extremely important sense, consistent with the affirmation of satisfaction that undergirds consumerism. The analysis in both cases indicates an acceptance that a model of man which defines us to be essentially utility maximizers or, more baldly stated, satisfaction chasers is correct in its main contours. We are, in both perspectives, implicitly reduced to veritable pleasure machines or satisfaction addicts feverishly searching for the next fix. The consumerists improve the quality of the stuff, pretest for adverse side-effects, label the dosage correctly, and hand out stiff criminal penalties to those who push it cut with impurities. Restraining ecologists frequently propose a solution akin to the cold-turkey cure. People must be restrained because if left to their devices, they will persist in consuming and polluting. In Nader, the consumer movement has discovered an ironically appropriate figure to lead the movement. He is unpleasurable and will not be diverted from performing the necessary work by those enticements which those who hold economic hegemony might offer. Similarly, some political ecologists would advocate the seating of a puritan at the controls of the environmental spaceship—that is, someone who can pull the plug on the satisfaction machine and interrupt the decadent push of the culture before we kill ourselves with too much pleasure. If only Nader was available full-time!

When they counterpose their conception of human nature to the magnitude of the threats we will likely confront, some political ecologists come frightfully close to telling us that the human swine needs to be coerced. Heilbroner even goes so far as to imply that given our past history, we may well enjoy it.[22] Yet good reasons should lead us to think that accepting a model of man which defines us primarily as pleasure-seeking egoists carries with it an unduly constricted political vision that may obscure more attractive options. We may certainly appear to be simply chasers after consumer satisfactions, but this may have much to do with the kinds of enjoyment available, the kinds of activity in which it is currently possible to engage, and the kind of activity that is systematically and structurally foreclosed than with human nature per se. If the argument in the previous section—which claimed that our desire to acquire consumer satisfactions is an understandable, though ultimately unsuccessful, attempt to obtain the freedom and autonomy that is not readily available in other realms of daily experience—is taken to be sensible, we have to scrutinize very carefully proposals which testify that even this conception of freedom must be disallowed. Without this skepticism, we can easily fail to consider other political issues which may significantly impinge on ecological dilemmas. The factory worker driving the Impala becomes the problem—not the conditions at his workplace. The working-class parents with five children are said to be in need of moral instruction, although the distribution of wealth in society remains as skewed as ever.

Ecologists have also avoided acknowledging Nader's descriptions of the victimizations which pervade our lives, and the failure to come to grips with his story represents an egregious intellectual failure. The assignment of an alternative life with no reference to the fears, anxieties, and daily realities of those for whom you are recommending the change signifies the worst sort of intellectual distancing. Furthermore, the strategic difficulties of building a political movement so negative in its emphases are probably overwhelming. This excessive negativity is not found in the desire to dismantle and rebuild political institutions (most revolutionary movements do exactly this), but in the realization that some political ecologists hold out to their following nothing more than a tentative promise of survival, assuming that we are not first destroyed in a thoroughly traditional manner.

The inadequacy of these political formulations should not, however, be translated into a general disdain for environmental matters. Many particulars of the environmental critique are well-argued and persuasive. So too is the reasonableness of what might be called the ecologists' wager. Such a wager contends that we should organize our lives according to the belief that we live in a finite world containing a limited supply of resources. If the presumption is correct, we stave off the social catastrophes that would be the possible consequences of ecological imbalancing. If it is incorrect, even though we have organized our lives as if it was true, we will not have diminished ourselves in the process so long as our choices were made freely and democratically.

A more appropriate explanation of our current predicament than has been offered by either Nader or the ecologists will note that the American consumer is presently impaled on the twin poles of victim and plunderer. This is to realize that the development of American culture and society has proceeded in such a manner that the characteristic act of asserting our freedom (acquiring consumer goods) is marked by the fear that we are being unjustly exploited (Nader's victim) and is also the action by which we become less autonomous and doubly vicitimized (connecting our identities to that required by the corporate state) and contribute to the decay of the life-world in which we move (the consumer as plunderer). A genuine consumer politics—a movement that addresses the full ramifications of individual, corporate, and governmental action in a consumer society—will not confine itself to a single component of this predicament. By connecting the consumer interest with the public good, Nader has ignored those elements about which he will have to speak in order to convince us that his is a public-interest movement. Political ecologists have well described the problems that may result from continued adherence to a prodigal conception of growth. Yet they too have been similarly partial in their analysis. One trouble with both perspectives might be found in their original depiction of our nature—a picture distressingly simple-minded in explaining our current habits and exploring our potentialities.

Reopening New Channels

I have argued to this point that Nader's efforts to unite consumerism with environmentalism conceals the radically diverging conceptions under-girding each movement in reference to desirable and acceptable forms of living. To note this inconsistency is not merely an exercise in drawing scholastic distinctions. At the root of the ecological argument is a behest to change our lives, obscuring this by building an expedient coalition dilutes the force of the argument. It has also been claimed that both consumerism and enviromentalism assume that our nature compels us to chase market satisfactions in a perpetual race. Consumerists remove the hidden obstacles, environmentalists shackle us before we reach the start-ing blocks. This chapter concludes with a set of recommendations that might help public-interest reformers to speak to all the problems of a consumer society. The attention will focus on Nader because of the detailed analysis of political ecology presented in Chapter Six.

A critical starting point would be to determine the proper scope of economic and consumer considerations in our lives. Hannah Arendt, Sheldon Wolin, and others performed invaluable work during the past twenty years by rediscovering and articulating a conception of the political which was not entirely defined by stratagems to further our economic interests.[23] They accomplished the introduction of a relatively new element into our political discourse by comparing classical Athenian democracy to the interest-group version which had become the conventional wisdom of the age. These writers emphasized the distinction made in the classical world between the economic (or the realm of the "necessary") and the political wherein matters were not ordinarily cluttered or distorted by the pursuit of personal financial interests. The relevance of this body of work becomes quite noticeable as dissatisfaction with the rewards of consumer society increases and as ecological limits to growth become probable. By showing us examples of societies in which politics functioned as a conscious method of self-definition, they laid the groundwork for a contemporary politics in which we might participate for reasons loftier than personal gain.

This is not to claim that the separation of the political and the economic can or should be maintained, but to argue that politics is best conceived when it is not held to be only a branch of economics. To be sure, the political arena is the proper location for settling matters of economic justice. Moreover, there is a genuine sense in which our demands qua economic man are connected to our quest for dignity and to our nature as human beings who can develop their capacities through social interaction. Think of the gestation period in the formation of labor unions in which workers first achieve minimal recognition by ownership of their rights to the material components of a decent life. Also, witness revolutionary movements in which land reform and some redistribution of wealth comprise the initial recognition that peasants have certain human rights also. What we need to investigate and learn about today is how we can create a politics that recognizes our economic needs but not only our economic interests. It must be a politics that can maintain a creative tension, if not reconcile desires for economic security with longings for meetings other than exchange relationships.

In specific reference to Nader and the consumer movement, at least two major alterations would have to be performed. The first is to state explicitly that consumer politics as presently constituted should occupy only a segment of our political life and not serve as the justification for it. Nobody would argue that consumers ought not to be protected in their rightful spheres, but Nader and his followers have yet to delineate these areas or advance a practical and political criticism of the belief that the mere existence of wants and needs warrants equal protection for all. The answer to these questions will, of course, always be tentative and unclear at points because principles of division will be elusive in complex and ambiguous situations. Yet it is clear that by equating the good citizen with the good consumer, Nader has ignored issues which a reformist politics must address—most especially those matters of economic class. If Nader is to convince us that his is a public-interest movement, he will need to think more deeply than he has to this day about the distribution of wealth and capital.

A second component of a revised consumer politics should be a reflexive or critical outlook on the activity of consuming itself. Consumer advocates would become wary of confining their energies to either case work in which people are aided with particular victimizations or to class-action work in the courts or national legislature. Reflexive consumer education will consist not only in developing the capacity to distinguish quality from defective merchandise but also in learning to discern when consumption is being advertised to gratify desires and relieve tensions in ways that the activity cannot possibly perform. Consumerists would work not only to reduce victimizations but to diminish the resort to consumption pursuits to solve dilemmas of fear, inadequacy, and self-worth. This would take us beyond liberal political action as it is presently construed and would call for Nader to connect his personal beliefs about the harmfulness of some consumption to his life as a political figure and to develop strategies to illustrate more worthwhile modes of living that few of us have shown the capacity to create.

Students of politics might focus their work on the worth of our various activities. Mill believed that it might be possible to arrange pleasures within a hierarchy of satisfaction. We might skip this rank of ordering of satisfactions and instead discuss what kind of activity is important for human beings who are not only market satisficers. This is especially important if we believe that we are relational at our very core and that our self-worth will depend upon recognition and affirmation by significant others. We might try to connect our findings and speculations to an evaluation of present social conditions and speak about what changes would be necessary in the organization of production, leisure, and politics to provide greater scope for the activities we deem unnecessarily limited. This might potentially allow us to picture the move from a consumer society to an environmentally viable society in a more attractive light than have the strict ecologists.

It is, however, another matter altogether to predict whether Nader will be willing and able to proceed with these suggestions. His grave concern for ecological matters might be considered a promising sign. Yet it seems more likely that Nader, a reformer who has taken liberalism to its boundaries, will be unable to move further along than he has already. His desire to be pragmatic, his insistence on considering the consumer to be the fundamental unit of political analysis and his reluctance to criticize American business in a manner that might cause disaffection among a number of his supporters will probably leave him as firmly wedded to his inconsistencies as ever. If Nader's public-interest reform is to have an enduring legacy of significance, it may be that it has coincided with times which demand that we think once again as public citizens who will need to discover ways of doffing our consumer identities to share public burdens equitably and times, too, which may permit others to see in the clearest and starkest light that which Nader only dimly perceives.

Chapter 5

Our First Crisis of Affluence

Perhaps one of the most significant lines of division between liberals and radicals is marked by their respective positions on desirable changes in advanced commercial societies. Liberals, for the most part, testify that corporate excesses should be relieved by instituting political reforms which adjust, not overturn, the prevailing economic relationships. Radicals contend that this tinkering is not an adequate reply to the inherent failures of corporate capitalism. They argue that gross economic inequities, a lamentable climate of human relationships, and a destructive attachment to the consumption ethic cannot be permanently remedied without a fundamental reordering of the economic system. By describing Nader's waffling on ecological matters (heartily dedicated to environmental preservation on one hand, but equally reluctant to speak about imposing restraints on practices that reinforce the consumption ethic), the previous chapter has outlined what I think to be the increasing relevance of a "radical" stance when a society becomes aware of the limits to industrial growth. America now seems to face a crisis of affluence in which resources are perceived to be sufficient to supply everyone with the material components of a decent life, but only if social and political arrangements encourage moderation in both expectations and in the personal and corporate consumption of goods.

The social construction of reality or the package of beliefs and material conditions whose interplay make for a crisis of affluence can be stipulated as follows.

1) Material resources are thought to be sufficiently plentiful (either now or in the near future), and productive capacity is thought to be sufficiently developed (either now or in the near future) to furnish a reasonable economic standard of living for all members of a given society at present or in the near future.
2) Material resources are not thought to be sufficiently plentiful (either now or in the near future) to supply this decent stan-

dard of physical existence to everyone if expectations continue
to rise and if allocation, distribution, and consumption decisions are not wisely made.

3) Persons uphold the political ideal that economic, educational,
and governmental institutions should work to ensure that accepted standard of material existence by guarding against the
reckless draining of the resource reservoir.

If the first condition is not met, the problem is that of absolute scarcity
and not abundance or affluence. While allocational and distributional
questions are not insignificant in this situation, accenting the expansion
of productive capability is an understandable development strategy for a
society to follow; indeed, in some instances, it may be preferable to allow
a highly skewed distribution of wealth than to enforce the socialization of
poverty. If stipulation number two is believed to be inaccurate, a crisis of
affluence does not exist (though discontent with other aspects of consumer societies, such as the manufacturing of relative scarcities, may be
eminently justifiable) because what is widely held to be a decent material
life is available to most everyone without upsetting the existing economic
framework. Finally, although conditions number one and two may hold,
a society may not experience the "crisis" because of the dominant belief
that the production, allocation, and consumption of resources should not
be a matter for political decision-making. A substantial and influential
body of citizens may believe that it is incumbent on individuals to fend for
themselves and that each person should be allotted no more and no less
than the fruits of whatever they can accumulate in the free market.

America has often been thought of as a land of economic abundance in
which every industrious person could extract a fair share of its wealth
through his labor. The belief was contained in Locke's political thought,
it motivated the immigration of economically hard-pressed Europeans, it
helped to shape a political system that was more concerned with not stifling economic initiative than with elaborating schemes for the even
distribution and consumption of resources, and it has remained part of
the social mythology of many Americans to this day. Yet the accuracy of
this characterization has been frequently belied by the concrete historical
struggles of America's residents whose lives were defined by a desperate
striving to obtain the necessities for physical survival. For many, owning a
small parcel of land has signified a constant dependence on an unpredict-
able climate and the uncontrollable vagaries of the market. The bountiful
frontier was only accessible to those who possessed an adventurous spirit
and were willing to negotiate a hazardous terrain with uncertain means of
transportation. Immigration to cities of industrial "affluence" meant the

subjection of one's family to the degrading regimen of factory time and grueling work at subsistence wages. In this experience of life in America, potential abundance was overshadowed by perpetual reminders of scarcity and the felt threat of impending pain. The branch of learning which had most faithfully and systematically reflected this perception of scarcity was economics. So long as affluence depended on remarkable good fortune in the marketplace or on a pioneering bent, we could not truthfully claim, in a strict economic construction, to have surmounted scarcity.[1]

The contention that abundance was really at hand did not enter mainstream American economic thought until the late nineteenth and early twentieth centuries. The German-educated economist Simon Nelson Patten has been credited with the introduction of this assumption into our economic discourse.[2] Patten was a liberal Social Darwinist who argued that economic theory and political life ought to be revised to account for the solution to the long-standing problem of production. He thought a new economic order could possibly be created to abolish poverty forever if consumer tastes could be modified in line with what our new productive capacity could supply most copiously. He believed that mitigating the harsh struggle for survival could eliminate bitter class conflict, allow us to pursue the higher interests of progressive human beings, and permit us to live with greater moral rectitude. Patten's contemporary, Thorstein Veblen, responded to these assertions with a bitter and trenchant negativity. His criticism was not that Patten was incorrect to believe that contemporary society possessed the means to alleviate poverty, but that such a *rational reordering* of society in accord with its newly acquired technical facility was impossible in a nation governed by the mores of business enterprise. Veblen maintained that the proclivity of human beings to make invidious comparisons with one another was nurtured by the captains of industry so as to preclude an equitable allocation and consumption of resources. He suggested that hope for making rational use of scientific advances rested with the subordination of both politics and business to the dictates of technical efficiency.

This chapter interprets the writings of Patten and Veblen as responses to our initial crisis of affluence—a situation at the turn of the century wherein resources were thought by these political economists to be sufficient to sustain the members of the community, yet requiring a political commitment that would foster the production of appropriate goods and heighten the rationality of consumption habits. Patten is illustrative of the liberal position which argues that social problems should be considered in a light that takes the capitalist form of production for granted. Veblen is the caustic radical who argues that the dilemmas are insoluble while the business mores reign. The former emphasizes both the multiple advantages that have accrued from capitalist organization and the possibility of cooperative action between workers and socially responsible capitalists. The latter considers this dangerous hokum, and instead stresses the deprivations consequent to the business organization of production, allocation, and consumption.

Three arguments are contained in the presentation of Patten's and Veblen's analysis of the politics of a sustainable society. The first is that Veblen was correct to criticize a liberal reformism that spoke of ordering production, allocation, and consumption reasonably without uprooting the psychological foundations of business societies. The second maintains that although Veblen's ironic commentary provides a persuasive assessment of liberal reformism's shortcomings, his recommendations proposing that we conform to a technological imperative are indicative of a misbegotten radicalism in which criticism of the invidious partnership between government and business also becomes a preemptive denial of our potential for creative and democratic collective action in meeting the crisis of affluence. My concluding assertion is that the unresolved dilemma evident in the work of these two authors remains with us today: how do we create a sustainable society without resorting to strategies that diminish our stature as human beings?

Sustaining the Pleasure Economy

Simon Patten's commentary on the possibilities for abundance was comprised of a theory of historical development, a description of the obstacles to be hurdled if progress was to occur, and an explanation of the methods that might be employed to overcome these hindrances. The theory of historical development posited that scarcity might be eliminated due to a more sagacious utilization of nature and because of advances in production technology. The principal obstacle to the eradication of poverty was the persistence of habitual behavior—especially consumption patterns—that was more appropriate to an age of scarcity than an epoch of relative abundance. The means by which these anachronistic traits could be modified consisted primarily of welfare state measures that would raise the lower class by using the state's revenues to fund educational programs. It should be noted, however, that Patten's intellectual steadfastness in believing our principal social problem to be that of adjusting our habits to abundance was not complemented by a similar consistency in his presentation of solutions. Although he never abandoned his belief in the propriety of some social welfare programs, he spoke glowingly in the middle of his career about the social potential of eugenics, and toward the end of his active life he wrote about the need for a heightened religious consciousness throughout the population.[3]

Patten's earliest work criticized the dominant assumptions of his economist predecessors and contemporaries. In *The Premises of Political Economy*, he sought to prove the deficiencies of Ricardo's work on rent, Malthus' theorems on population, Mill's position on the relation of rent to wages, and the conventional wisdom on the merits of free trade. The most common weapon in his critical arsenal was the claim that these writers had enshrined as eternal laws of scarcity what were essentially matters of public opinion and alterable social organization. Previous economists had been blind to nature's potential because they had not been sensitized to the remarkable variety of goods available. "The real cause of the present social distress is to be found in the prevailing sentiment regarding the consumption of wealth, and especially of food. Nature is not equally productive of all kinds of wealth, and men cannot expect to choose those forms of wealth of which nature is least productive and receive the same reward as if they chose for consumption those articles supplied most abundantly by nature. Men complain of the niggardliness of nature when really the only thing wrong is the universal disposition on the part of men to prefer those forms of wealth of which nature is least productive, instead of other commodities of which nature offers a generous supply."[4] Although *The Premises* concluded with an assertion that modern society was a mixed blessing because a leveling process followed when conditions were upgraded to permit others than the fittest to prosper, Patten's later work declared that we must nevertheless pursue the *possibilities* of abundance with as much energy as could be mustered.

Patten's theory of history and the place of abundance within it was clearly reflected in his monograph *The Consumption of Wealth*. In this work, Patten maintained that we had entered a transition age in which society could move from relative scarcity to relative abundance or, as he was wont to put it, from a pain to a pleasure economy. In the past, according to Patten's reading of history, we ate and drank as much as possible in good times in order to store the reserves in our body that helped to ward off starvation in the lean weeks that invariably followed. Gluttony, for instance, contributed to survival and was a habit to be rationally encouraged because "the primitive man needed a strong appetite to withstand the hardships that an irregular food supply caused him to undergo."[5] Patten averred that the creation of a more or less steady food supply so that the "means of subsistence have become so regular that the average man never keenly feels the pangs of hunger" was the radical achievement of the modern age.[6]

This achievement permitted, according to Patten, a reordering of our consumption behavior in a beneficial manner. Patten had explained consumption patterns according to the rational workings of the laws of utility or according to the relations of pleasures to pains. He argued that our consumption was not principally dependent on what goods provided the most pleasure, but, most significantly, on what goods offered the most advantageous ratio of pleasures to pains. Patten frequently made his point by employing the example of the choice of dishes we might select at a free meal. He suggested that a rational person would choose the item he relished the most and, when satiated with this article, then proceed to consume the plate that offered the second highest quantity of pleasure. Yet this "natural" order of consumption exhibited at the free lunch was not equivalent to the economic order of consumption followed in everyday life. Imagine, Patten wrote, the selections that would be made if the diner was asked to pay for his choices, either by direct cash outlay or indirectly in labor hours. In all likelihood, these would be distinct from the natural order in evidence at the free meal because "our natural desire for an article is modified by the amount of labor required to produce it."[7] Modern agricultural production had succeeded in revising the traditional economic calculus of pleasures to pains. Goods that were once dear had been substantially cheapened and could become a regular component of our standard of living.

Patten maintained in *The Consumption of Wealth* that the transition to a pleasure economy, if left to natural evolution, would be harsher than warranted by the state of social technology. The transition would be marred by a displacement of the lower class and the persistence of conditions which any civilized person would necessarily deplore. He believed that economic abundance could be used to humanize the inexorable path of laissez-faire Social Darwinism. "The fact that improved production will in the end cure its own evils, does not relieve society from the obligation to work for the same end."[8] He argued that a general concern for the well-being of one's fellows was a moral imperative. "In aiding the development of the lower classes, rather than allowing them to be destroyed in the struggle for existence, the motive should be a love of humanity and not the necessities of social progress. There need be no fear that society will cease to progress. The problem is to shorten the period of transition as much as possible, and to bring as large a proportion as possible of our present population into harmony with the environment."[9]

The pleasure economy, in Patten's most optimistic description, would give average persons access to quality goods, would allow individuals to move up the hierarchy of satisfactions, and would simplify the dilemmas of moral action. Production on a large scale enabled us to partake of enjoyments previously reserved for the decidedly affluent. This was noticeable in the dispersion of art and in the growth of the clothing industry. The process of photographic reproduction had become so advanced that "everywhere the homes of the poorest people are filled with beautiful objects, many of which had no cost."[10] He noted a similar effect in the fashion industry. The average laborer could now purchase off-the-rack garments of the most becoming character that could not be distinguished by the untrained eye from the tailored garments of corporate executives.

Residents of the pleasure economy were also fortunate, for they had escaped the strictures of past morality. To support this thesis, Patten first attempted to illustrate the moral relevance of economics and then tried to demonstrate how economic science's calculus of pleasure facilitated ethical decision-making. He defended his initial proposition by arguing that ethical tenets must conform to physical or economic conditions. Anyone who assayed to establish an absolute ethics without reference to environmental variation succeeded in proposing a moral standard which "may be a very good one on Jupiter or Mars, but certainly is not fitted for our world."[11] Economics rendered moral choices less exacting via its demonstration that the existing condition of the external world could be radically modified. Morality in the pleasure economy would occur by savoring the enjoyments one would receive from performing the correct action rather than simply dreading the consequences of an improper action. The asceticism and renunciation of primitive morals could be supplanted by the variety of ethically laudable activities available to the modern man. "It is therefore possible to impute to any act a source of pleasure greater than can be derived from violating the moral principle."[12]

Patten attempted to establish his assertion that the alteration of external conditions tempered the demands of conscience by reference to the moral calculus involved in the consumption of alcohol. In a pain economy, the intake of alcohol was the source of intense pleasure, a catalyst to immoral action, and a means of self-pollution and destruction. To guarantee that one might avoid the negative repercussions of its consumption, an individual was compelled to renounce the pleasures of alcohol altogether. The abstention by which one purchased continued health came at the price of less satisfying consumption. Patten maintained that the economic order of consumption in the modern economy had created the preconditions for receiving a greater measure of pleasure than that yielded by strong liquors—pleasures that were not typically accompanied by deleterious side-effects. The rational individual would consume a variety of foods and beverages that were unquestionably more enjoyable than crude alcoholic beverages. The selection of the moral option in a pleasure economy would thus be "easy as it is for a capitalist with his savings instinct properly developed to choose the best form of production when the choice involves greater or smaller amounts of capital."[13] Because economic abundance resulted in less demanding moral conundrums, Patten concluded by advising ethical reformers that "whoever would make mankind moral in a natural way must make his beginning and get his mechanism into operation in the economic world."[14]

But the mere existence of physical abundance did not entail for Patten a successful and rapid transition to the ways of the pleasure economy. Patten expounded a theory of social heredity in which—despite the altered economic conditions—we were collectively influenced by the experiences of the age of scarcity. The problem of collective heredity was that our habits and appetites were firmly embedded in those unconscious assumptions about the environment that our recent technological progress had already invalidated. "The obstacles to a rapid improvement in mankind do not lie in the present environment. The habits and appetites of man were formed in the environment of the distant past. Human nature becomes so adjusted to this environment that it clings to the old and distrusts the new. . . . The harmony between ourselves and the environment has been disturbed. We have built a new mansion on the hill but still prefer the cottage in the valley."[15] The increase in production did not signify a necessary end to scarcity because if we continued to consume in the same manner as we had previously—with strong appetites and untutored diets—we would return to hard times. Nondiscriminating appetites endangered everyone. "The desire for rare articles is the direct outcome of vigorous appetites. The demand for liquor and tobacco keeps the supply of food and clothing at a minimum. The simple vegetables are set aside for meats and other condensed foods. The more common parts of the animal are neglected for some rare portion, and wild game and animals are preferred to domestic breeds. In these, and many other ways, strong appetites reduce the food supply to the narrowest limits, and bring on a conflict between the increase in population and the means of subsistence."[16] Unless appetites were modified, increased production of the food supply might result in the increased consumption of the same article or the use of the improved supply merely to feed an expanding population. In either manner, the technical capacity for prosperity would be undermined and the population returned to cyclical scarcity.

The methods which Patten proposed to deal with this issue were those which might today be considered welfare state plans. He believed that the state needed to take an active role in deciding to what uses the social surplus should be directed. Patten's welfare state was consciously paternalistic, but he contended that such noblesse oblige was the only responsible method for instituting a progressive society. "It is now too late to expect that a better consumption of wealth will come of itself to the lower classes. With every step in social progress, more of this free education will be needed, if the weaker portions of society are to be led along the road the more progressive have already traversed. Society must adopt a vigorous educational policy, or shut its eyes while the destructive tendencies of modern civilization slowly force the weak and unwary into a life of misery and vice."[17] Patten also argued that the laboring classes were entitled to special consideration because modern conditions were not such as to permit the upward mobility of the past, and even people of quality might not be given the opportunity to prove their mettle. "I think also, the laboring classes have a claim on society, due to the peculiar circumstances which now impede their progress to a much greater extent than formerly. Production on a small scale and a low price for land afford remarkable inducement for savings. The smaller producer readily finds opportunity to secure a large return for his labor, in a way that will develop his ability and skill. Under present conditions, it takes a much more able man than formerly to seize right opportunities to enable him to pass from the laboring to the employing class."[18]

The establishment of a welfare state, in Patten's mind, was preferable to the course of action endorsed by the socialists—that of class conflict. Patten's belief in this respect was prompted by a number of reasons. First, Patten felt that the proletariat had demonstrated no special commitment to virtuous actions. Second, he thought that socialists who believed that class conflict could improve the condition of the lower classes were empirically mistaken. If not afforded a strong measure of paternal aid, would not the lower classes inevitably be eliminated in the struggle for existence? Patten's reading of Darwin convinced him of a fundamental misperception by Marx in the portrayal of a class-based revolutionary movement. Darwinism did not prove that the "world belongs to rabbits. It proves that rabbits belong to foxes."[19] Third, Patten contended that socialists misjudged both the historical record of capitalist organization and the likely direction it would take in the future (voluntary socialism). Patten maintained that since the time of Marx, capitalist production had reduced the suffering from sheer physical want and had solidified the stability of industry. Furthermore, it has been characterized by a social responsiveness that had "demonstrated the power of voluntary social organization and justified the hopes of Adam Smith and Robert Owen."[20] The problems which remained in society were ones in which "our foes are not groups of antagonistic men, but incompetence, mismanagement and maladjustment."[21] Finally, Patten believed that emphasizing the categories of social class and endorsing conflict as an engine for change was a reversion to politics appropriate to a pain economy. The qualities associated with particular social classes indicated what these groupings were lacking in the full complement of human capacities. The lower class lacked the civilizing traits necessary for leading the appropriate life within the pleasure economy, while the rich did not possess the necessary sympathy for the plight of the impoverished that would be manifested in genuinely compassionate souls. Pitting these groupings against one another could not eliminate the problems which made conflict appear to be a reasonable course of action.

Pecuniary Culture and the Denial of Abundance

Patten's belief that abundance was at hand and might possibly be achieved through the active cooperation of the members of his society was not shared by all his contemporaries. Many neglected to address his central thesis and instead remarked on particular elements.[22] The maverick economist Thorstein Veblen comprehended Patten's intentions but was by no means convinced that the latter's presentation was accurate. Veblen commented specifically about the inaccuracy of Patten's theory of historical development. There ran throughout the body of Veblen's work, too, an implicit denial of the possibility of cooperative action by the capitalists in the spirit of the public interest. Patten's historical naivete, in Veblen's analysis, was only equaled by a failure to grasp the ineluctable workings of commercial society. The reservations which Patten occasionally expressed about the future direction of business operations became, in Veblen's hands, sufficient reason to aver that capitalists could never make optimal use of their expanded productive capability.

Veblen believed that Patten's historical analysis expounding a rationalistic, developmental model of evolution was a fictional recreation of our tradition not supported by the historical record. He maintained that the sharp distinction contained in Patten's work between a pleasure and a pain economy was a logical distinction which "served no useful purpose in social analysis."[23] Veblen remarked that in describing the latter mode of economic organization, Patten had casually dispensed with the mound of evidence that anthropologists had unearthed in their study of primitive societies. According to Veblen, Patten had characterized the pain economy as a social setting in which "fear and the avoidance of pain are the prominent motives for action. The sensory ideas are so grouped that they give early intimation of the presence of every possible evil or foe. . . . Man must have an intrinsic fear of evil."[24] Veblen believed that the primitives did not operate according to such rationalistic criteria. The rituals and superstitions of the primitives led them, in Veblen's mind, to embrace "patent evils while the demons and spirits which the primitives took fastidious care to avoid were for the most part figments."[25]

Veblen's dismay with Patten's description of the pain economy was part of his more inclusive criticism that Patten's tendency to compartmentalize history into specific epochs led him to overlook the human traits which were recognizable under almost every material condition. "That continuity of tradition and folklore, as well as that persistence of physical type and temperament, seemed to have passed harmless over Mr. Patten."[26] The implication of Veblen's derisiveness was that Patten's description of the pain economy was paralleled by an equally invalid characterization of the incipient pleasure economy. If the former was not as loathesome and fearful as Patten sought to portray it, the coming pleasure economy would not, of necessity, augur beneficial for mankind. The traits formed in pre-pecuniary societies did not dissipate as the environment was modified, and Veblen was emphatic that the traits peculiar to capitalist organization engendered more costs than benefits.

These two themes—the persistence of old irrational habits only cloaked in modern form and the destructiveness endemic to a society run by and for business—were contained in the corpus of Veblen's work. Both themes were clearly articulated in his famous commentary on the leisure classes. He first strove to explain the link between modern society and more traditional social organizations. He claimed that the older habits of emulation and conspicuous leisure were discernible but in altered form within business societies. Under the modified environmental conditions, the conspicuous leisure of the master was noticeable in the conspicuous leisure of the middle-class wife. "It is by no means an uncommon spectacle to find a man applying himself to work with the utmost assiduity, in order that his wife may in due form render him the degree of vicarious leisure which the common sense of the time demands."[27] Veblen further explained that the conditions peculiar to commercial societies were developing in such a manner that the mere demonstration of leisure did not provide a fully adequate sign of one's worth. The changing mode of production and the diffuseness of everyday life had torn people away from established communities wherein conspicuous leisure was easily noticed and duly honored. In a nation of strangers, Veblen contended that the quintessential demonstration of one's status was an "unremitting ability to pay."

This signified that the education an individual received from the dominant institutions would not be, as Patten had hoped, to the requirements of a sustainable state, but would instead be to the monetary canons of decency. The energies and paychecks of the majority of the population would go to obtain these goods which had been defined as necessary for a normal existence. "For the great body of people in any modern community, the proximate ground of expenditure in excess of what is required for physical comfort is not a conscious effort to excel in the expensiveness of their visible consumption, so much as it is a desire to live up to the conventional standards of decency in the amount and grade of goods consumed."[28] This system of monetary emulation disengaged the productive apparatus from any presumed social responsibility to distribute and consume goods reasonably; indeed, Veblen believed that this possibility would be forever neglected as long as we lived under the reign of the "captains." He agreed with Patten that our foes were incompetence and mismanagement, but maintained that these adversaries were embodied in the concrete personages of the captains of industry.

The growth and transformation of the advertising industry at the outset of the twentieth century provided a fitting example of the captains' propensity to make profitable use of our irrational habits rather than employ our technical proficiency to pursue the more laudable end of social justice. Patten had worried on occasion that excessive consumption desires and unscrupulous advertising might hinder the proper adaptation to abundance. Veblen, infinitely more critical of business culture, was convinced that the transformation of advertising exemplified the incapacity of commercial societies to de-emphasize the irrationality of past behavior.

> In its elements, of course, sales publicity is nothing new. But its eventual working out under absentee ownership has disclosed a character and significance beyond anticipation and beyond ancient example. Yet much of the doctrinal matter that goes into print in behalf of yeast-cakes, style-plus clothing, lipsticks, face-creams and the like still reads not unlike that ancient achievement in publicity the royal preamble to the code of Hammurabi, said to date from the Twenty-First Century B.C. There is in both the same diligent attention to overstatement and the same unfailing avoidance of all that is to be said in abatement."[29]

Salesmanship, in this new milieu, functioned to routinize and publicize the standards of taste and reputability. A society of strangers required an effective mechanism for disseminating the appropriate values of business societies; advertising performed this service admirably.

Furthermore, the techniques utilized in the advertising process were geared not only to sell every product that could potentially be marketed, but to produce a routinized body of consumers that could be expected to purchase the products of business. "But very much as is true with mechanical industry, so also in large-scale publicity, what one concern with ample funds can do, another concern with funds in the same amplitude in the same or another line of manufacturing can do just as well."[30] The consequence of these standardized advertising practices was the "fabrication of consumers, . . . perfectly equivalent to the other products of machine industry as regards the quality, rate and volume of output."[31] This fabrication of consumers, of mechanical bodies to supply the profit margins, was the perfect illustration of the contradiction that had emerged between the technical proficiency of the industrial engineers and the wastefulness of the capitalist system. "Salesmanship is the most conspicuous and perhaps the gravest of these wasteful and industrial futile practices that are involved in the businesslike conduct of industry: it bulks large both in its immediate costs and in its meretricious consequences, . . . and while the proportion of sales-costs to production-costs goes on increasing, the cost of living continually increases for the underlying population, and business-like necessities continue to enlarge the necessary expenditures on the ways and means of salesmanship."[32]

Veblen argued that business routinely engaged in sabotage or "something in the way of retardation, withdrawal, unemployment of plant and efficiency—whereby production is kept short of capacity," in order to retain profit margins.[33] He believed, unlike Patten, that the captain of industry was incidental to the expansion of the American economy, a growth that should have been attributed to an advance in the state of the industrial arts. Individual entrepreneurs merely utilized the tools which had become more refined and sophisticated over the course of time. "The state of the industrial art is the joint stock of knowledge derived from past experience, and is held and passed on as an indivisible possession of the community at large. It is the indispensable foundation of all productive industry, but except for certain minute fragments . . . this joint stock is no man's individual property."[34] The most valuable contribution that an individual entrepreneur could make would be to stand aside and permit the level of the productive arts to advance.

Veblen believed that there certainly was no compelling judgment, even if the dubious assumption that there ever was one was granted, for rewarding capitalistic talents in the contemporary age. Financial management entailed following standardized procedures and the measures which conduced to the competent direction of an efficient enterprise could be best performed by less speculative souls. Further, Veblen maintained that businessmen were directing their enterprises in such a slipshod manner that they were demonstrating their "industrial incompetence in a progressively convincing manner."[35] Inefficiencies and inconsistencies could be discerned throughout the entire operation because the entrepreneur frequently "let well enough alone" if a profit was consistently turned. "The common good, so far as it is a question of material welfare, is evidently best served by an unhampered working of the industrial system at its full capacity without interruption or dislocation. But it is equally evident that the owner or manager of any given concern or section of this industrial system may be in a position to gain something for himself at the cost of the rest by obstructing, retarding or dislocating this working system at some critical point in such a way as will enable him to get the best of the bargain in his dealings with the rest."[36]

The efficiency of the productive apparatus had been further reduced by political meddling in the affairs of industry on the behalf of business. "Politics and investment are still allowed to decide matters of industrial policy which should plainly be left to the general staff of production engineers driven by no commercial bias."[37] Critical political goals such as the elimination of poverty and full employment could only be realized if politicians became mindful of the negative consequences that were the typical upshots of their interference. Moreover, political power was used to support the legitimacy of the vested interests by making it legal for these interests to get "something for nothing." A protective tariff, in Veblen's mind, was "that method of taxing the common man for the benefit of the vested interests" which was, in short, simply a "larcenous use of the national establishment."[38] The most disturbing element of American politics for Veblen was not the particular uses of political authority to uphold the right of business prodigality, but the ideological underpinnings of American politics which attested to an individual's right to self-determination while actually granting unlimited freedom to the forces which naturally undermined it. In Veblen's mind, individual rights had become mere formalities in the face of the reality of business dominance. "The great distinguishing mark of the common man is that he is helpless within the rules of the game as it is played in the Twentieth Century under the enlightened principles of the Eighteenth Century."[39] The cooperation that Patten had advocated between the state and the capitalists only reinforced the destructive tendencies of business societies and did not work for the benefit of the common person.

The Technological Imperative

The solution Veblen advocated to rid society of its pervasive inefficiencies was a general purge of the industrial and political spheres: replace the captains in the executive suites with those who could manipulate a slide rule and deny the validity of political arithmetic in industrial matters. Although Veblen had earlier mouthed populist rhetoric, by the 1920s he was convinced that the single thread of hope remaining for mankind was that the populations of industrial societies might acknowledge the necessity of bowing to the superior wisdom of technological rationality and elevate a coterie of technologists—supplemented by a corps of insightful economists—to a ruling directorate. These were the only men capable of divorcing rational judgment from profit-orientation and superstition.

> By training and perhaps also by native bent, the technologists
> find it easy and convincing to size up men and things in terms
> of tangible performance without commercial afterthought,
> except so far as their apprenticeship to the captains of finance
> may have made commercial afterthought a second nature to
> them. Many of the younger generation are beginning to under-
> stand that engineering begins and ends in the realm of tangible
> performance and that commercial expediency is another
> matter. . . . to these men who are trained in the stubborn logic
> of technology, nothing is quite real that cannot be stated in the
> realm of tangible performance.[40]

The logical possibility that revolutionary action could be initiated by the technologists was not precluded by their relatively insignificant numbers. By controlling the actual means of the nation's livelihood, they were endowed with a practical importance far in excess of their numerical size, and the conditions under which they labored were conducive to the successful completion of the imperative task of political organization. The technologists were rational men whose work further instructed them in the value of cause-and-effect thinking which, in another form, might be translated into discovering the most effective methods of political action. Veblen also claimed that the class consciousness of the technicians differed from that of society's extant groupings in that it often transcended the self-interest of other classes. "They are thrown into position as responsible directors of the industrial system, and by the same move they are in a position to become arbiters of the community's material welfare. They are becoming class conscious and they are no longer driven by a commercial interest in the sense in which the syndicated owners and the federated workmen are vested interests."[41] The progress of society did not thus depend on the development of altruism by the engineers but merely on a correct assessment of their vocational interests. Gains would accrue to all through the beneficent work of technological advance. The invisible hand of the market was to be replaced by the invisible hand of technological advance.

Veblen believed that the substitution of the technicians for the workers as the engine of political change was warranted on both practical and epistemological grounds. He argued that the laboring class could not be realistically considered the vanguard of any revolutionary movement because of its political disposition in the present, its likely docility in the future, and its epistemological relation to the means of production. Veblen echoed Lenin when he argued that labor organizations reflected, at best, a trade union consciousness. "They are apparently moved by the feeling that so long as the established arrangements are maintained they will come in for a little something over and above what would come to them if they were to make common cause with the undistinguished common lot. In other words, they have a vested interest in a narrow margin of preference over and above what goes to the common man."[42] Nor did Veblen believe that this state of affairs was likely to change in the foreseeable future. The workers were temporarily indisposed to vigorous action, and the population could be expected to tolerate incompetent leadership indefinitely. But the most important consideration in Veblen's explanation of working-class revolutionary inadequacy was its technological incompetence. Veblen did not believe that the proletariat possessed either the technical or the management skills required to direct effectively a complex society. A successful revolution of workers, if such a miracle could be woven, would only result in anarchy and a severe dislocation of the country's industrial capacity. "In effect it is a question of whether the discretion and responsibility in the management of the country's industry shall pass from the financiers, who speak for the vested interests, to the technicians who speak for the industrial system as a going concern. There is no third party qualified to make a colorable bid or qualified to make good its pretensions."[43]

The advantages of instituting the regime of the technocrats resided in the benefits that would accrue to the population from efficient management. If capitalist organization reinforced inefficient traits by adding layers to the problems of our primitive condition, the attraction of technological innovation adhered in its promise not only to undermine the profit system, but in its potential to overcome the foolishness which had become embedded in human nature. As the population internalized the machinelike quality of rationality (Veblen believed that as the workers became disciplined to the rhythms of the machine and the demands of clockwork they would learn these qualities), the range and extent of destructive emulation described in the *Leisure Class* might be lessened. We could become less swayed by the deceptive practices of business enterprise which conveyed only symbolic reassurances and more capable of judging events and persons in terms of tangible performance. By removing the captains from their position of influence, the common stock of technological knowledge could be fully utilized to mitigate poverty in and across nations and break the connection between politics and the vested interests.

Veblen's chapter in *The Engineers and the Price System* entitled "A Memorandum on a Practicable Soviet of Technicians" outlined the proper relationship between the technicians and the underlying class. While he believed that the laboring classes were incompetent to manage the industrial system wisely, he likewise understood that their support for his alternative was indispensable. His answer was to suggest that the technicians work to "engineer consent." But so long as they have not, at least, "the tolerant consent of the population at large, backed by the aggressive support of the trained working force engaged in transportation and in the greater primary industries, they will be substantially helpless to set up a practicable working organization on the new footing."[44] The educational campaign to seduce the population to grant the necessity for the technical management of industry was best supplemented by a genuine concern for the community's material welfare. Popular approval would be gained with the creation of a materially satisfied citizenry.

Veblen did not, to be sure, exude a resolute confidence that such a radical break with the existing organization of industry could be negotiated in his lifetime. Despite the presentation of an occasional optimistic scenario, Veblen normally maintained that the captains had succeeded in inculcating their values throughout the population to a degree that was probably irreversible. Not only the working class, but the technicians—the real force of society—had deferred to the voice of business enterprise. The forthcoming years were not likely to be an era of abundance but a time of "continued and increased shame and confusion, hardship and dissension, unemployment and privation, waste and insecurity of person and property."[45] If the absentee owners were to be replaced, the impetus for the event would more likely be an abdication of the captains due to a complete inability to handle the complex industrial apparatus with a sufficient degree of facility, than it would from a revolutionary putsch of the technicians. It was only absolute necessity that would tutor the human animal in the efficient logic of existence.

Yet Veblen's intellectual commitment to a technologically oriented society was seriously flawed on more than pragmatic grounds. He neither understood the compatibility between business mores and the requirements of technical society, nor was he sufficiently critical of the human problems that such a society would invariably generate. So quick to draw the distinction between the operation of business and the efficient logic of technology, Veblen was not equally adroit at fathoming the connections that might be forged between the two. As a result of his dichotomizing, Veblen was unable to accurately characterize the relationship between the impetus toward profit and the efficient working of industry. In Veblen's mind, technology was efficient, business not, the former redounded to the benefit of humanity, the latter to the vested interests. But a compatibility that escaped Veblen's analysis does exist between the business management of industry and the technical mode of production. Veblen was plainly mistaken to believe that the consumer goods where were the output of business production would not be attractive to the workers in a technicalized society; indeed, a partial rationalization of the work environment can reinforce the desire for consumer acquisitions which business societies routinely generate. Individuals need to find sources of fulfillment. If their work-life is rendered humdrum, one can turn to consumer goods as the most readily available source of pleasure. The acquisition of these products, as we have seen, serve a wide range of purposes. These may be perceived as the justification for conforming to the rhythms of the machine or as the manner of obtaining autonomy not available in other areas of life. The growth of technology can surely bolster the desirability of the products of business. The flourishing black market in consumer goods and the efforts of nominally socialist nations to produce more are illustrative. The production of consumer goods is the means by which the price system retains its loyal cadre of workers while appropriating their minds.

Perhaps Veblen's most serious weakness was his reluctance to adopt a critical perspective on the transformation of the instinct of workmanship in the modern age. He had attributed to mankind an "instinct to perform valuable work in a proficient manner under circumstances of moderate exigence."[46] This instinct was usually directed toward the goal of increasing technical efficiency and enlarging the common stock of technological knowledge available to mankind. Yet the defining feature of the modern era was that the common pool of knowledge was accessible to just a few highly trained people. While the work instinct was becoming increasingly sophisticated, the personal competence and the craft skill of the ordinary worker was atrophying. Veblen was too willing to accept this tradeoff which he believed was integral to the industrial mode of production. He endorsed an accommodation to the machine because he felt that the loss of personal competence was balanced by an increase in machinelike rationality which might substantially improve our material welfare. Better to be disciplined and well-off than skilled, impoverished, and foolish. If the choice was either the discipline of the machine or the comfort of the occult, Veblen embraced the former and banished the irrational. Our problem with Veblen is that the proportions of the choice might not be as fixed as he thought.

Patten, Veblen and a Sustainable Society

Simon Patten was the first American economist to notice the potential of abundance in a systematic way. Significantly, Patten's conception of abundance was frugal when judged by contemporary standards. His notion of plenty denoted the systemic capacity to provide the material sustenance that would enable everyone to live without the fear of descending to absolute poverty. Because the full capability of the industrial apparatus was not apparent to Patten, he was compelled to speak about "proper consumption" and the imposition of judicious restraints on the untutored desires of his fellows. In his articles about the economic foundations of morality, Patten argued that the proper limits might be established by an education to genuine pleasure. If we could learn to make the correct imputation of utilities consistently or to make an economically sound calculation of pleasure and pain, we could restrict the consumption desires that were both detrimental to our personal well-being and inimical to the progress of society. The progressive man learned to enjoy a variety of pleasures by consuming a small amount of an assortment of goods and by ejecting discordant elements from the arrangement. The discordant elements were, in Patten's theories, those which he deemed personally destructive and socially wasteful. The magic and ingenuity of his solution lay in the assertion that the *restraints* were imposed through a more knowledgeable pursuit of *pleasure.*

Patten did not, however, succeed in describing the process by which the population might distinguish between genuine and inconvenient pleasures and be persuaded to consume the appropriate goods. His effort to speak about the imposition of restraints was not only simplified in his mind but was also undermined in practice by an uncritical evaluation of commercial society's development. His claim denying the validity of ideological struggles, whether these be fought through violent upheavals or contests in the electoral arena, was established by attributing the problems of adjusting to abundance primarily to the ignorance of the masses. By depoliticizing the captain of industry and depicting his activity in a highly positive manner, Patten blinded himself to the likely consequences of a capitalist economic framework that was antithetical to his conception of limits. Patten did not comprehend the difficulty of upholding an ethic of public-spiritedness and collective sharing in a society wherein the acquisition of commodities is the chief avenue for obtaining satisfaction. His goal of attaining a state where people were encouraged to pursue the "higher interests" was ultimately contradicted by a fundamental acceptance of market societies in their presently constituted form.

Thorstein Veblen was demonstrably more attuned to the core deficiencies of market organization than Patten. Veblen thought market society was an irrational social system that did not guarantee the material welfare of its residents. He argued that what ensued from capitalist organization was neither worthy of praise nor likely to sustain everyone. He believed that market societies fostered such an array of wants that the citizens could never be materially contented as long as the capitalist structure remained intact. Veblen, writing when affluence had just become a possibility, was more concerned with expanding production than with limiting it. Yet, he was always ready to note that both this goal and that of decreasing emulation was dependent on altering the basic tendencies of business societies. A sustainable society—one that could produce, allocate, and consume resources wisely—could not be formed without discarding the commodity fetishism of market societies.

The power of Veblen's analysis was diminished, however, by his endorsement of technological rationality. He presented us with a Hobson's choice of accommodating ourselves to the discipline of the machine or to continue with the iniquitous functioning of capitalist organization. Empirically, he mistook the extent of the compatibility between technological organization and the price system. Normatively, he mistook the desirability of conforming to the discipine of the machine. His acceptance of the bargain left us only to be robots for whom the state provides material welfare. Productive and fulfilling work had vanished in Veblen's world because we sacrificed personal competence for the greater advance of the industrial system. Symbolic interaction disappeared as we learned to think solely in terms of cause and effect. Public life and political action became irrelevant as the items normally considered subject to common deliberation were handled efficiently by a select few. Veblen established the community of man by denying all that was inherently human.

Patten's dilemma of discovering the methods of limiting consumption has returned to confound American liberals with the advent of ecological problems. Having come to depend on the growth economy and a provision of a variety of consumer goods as a backdrop to their strivings to implement measures of economic and moral reform, liberals simply deferred reckoning with the issues that occupied Patten—even though this reticence also meant silence in respect to Veblen's comments on the desirability of a consumer society. The abandonment can be seen in the directions followed by "consumer politics" in recent times. Patten spoke repeatedly, if often wrongheadedly, about the attributes and place of "proper" consumption in a progressive society. Those concerned with the consumer interest today speak almost exclusively in terms of protecting the consumer from the machinations of corporate enterprise and only at rare moments do they offer a qualitative assessment of consumer society.

Currently faced with a crisis of affluence, progressive reformers and the more reflective members of the Democratic party are in a practical bind. Because they have not challenged the prevailing wisdom regarding the desirability of a consumer economy, needs and desires have multiplied to keep pace with the expansion of production, so that cries of economic distress are still loud. Although this distress has always been an objective reality for many, it is a perception shared by members of the middle-class. It is not at all unusual to hear college professors moan about the difficulties of getting along on their incomes. On the other hand, there is the sober realization that even after acknowledging these problems of inflation, our resource consumption testifies that we are leading a recklessly extravagant life. No pat formulas which can alleviate these problems are available to activists because proposed solutions frequently run at cross-purposes. Liberal politicians and reformers have tried to obviate the more disturbing symptoms of each issue without a comprehensive statement of the directions we ought and perhaps need to follow. If it is not empirically accurate to claim that there has been an end to liberalism, one can assuredly state that it is fragmented. Liberalism has become a politics of patches, plugs, and bubble-gum as its votaries scurry to repair the cracks and leaks which multiply faster than they can be fixed.

This practical evidence of the failure of liberalism cannot be entirely comforting even to those who have been forecasting its decline for a number of years. The consequences of its inadequacy may be neither pleasing nor benign, for the potential responses may only function to diminish our capacity to create a humanly worthwhile society. Polarization, intense bitterness, and more severe use of the government's authority could possibly become the standard political fare. Those of us who have aspired to escape the strictures of liberal utilitarianism must confess that many of our assumptions were rooted in the suburban idea of abundance that no longer seems reasonable. The works of Michael Harrington and Herbert Marcuse are certainly manifestations. The task before us today is not to maintain that even Patten's frugal abundance is not still with us, but to demonstrate that the worthwhile elements of the liberal tradition need not be sacrificed to a politics of survival.

Chapter 6

Recycling Hobbes: The Limits to Political Ecology

I remember quite vividly my introduction to the ecology movement. It occurred at an antiwar rally that I attended when I was nineteen and only politicized in a piecemeal fashion. I was conversing with a couple of friends, and upon entering the main speaking area, we passed a young couple holding what was, at least for me, an unusual placard. The first half of their sign urged us to be more supportive of all life and to become more attuned to the natural rhythms of the cosmos. The other section noted that environmental deterioration could only be halted if we made a conscious decision to change our lives. I had been angered, prior to this experience, by the systematic American destruction of the Vietnamese environment, but I had not been personally sensitized to the destructive ramifications of our everyday, normal behavior patterns. Since that day I have never failed to associate ecological concern with the memory of that couple and the urging of their message. Even more, however, I associate environmental politics with the experiences of the era—particularly the festive celebration of life that these gatherings occasionally inspired and the participatory ethos which infused the better aspects of sixties politics.

The actual politics of environmental concern has followed an erratic course. Although an increasing number of people have become troubled by ecological dilemmas to the point where these problems are more frequently dealt with in our legislative chambers, no single outlook could be said to underlie the politics of environmental activists. In fact, many of our citizens most attuned to ecological issues have withdrawn from conventional politics in order to devote their energies to living a more austere and environmentally viable life within self-selected communities. Nor is agreement concerning what should be done about these pressing issues to be found among those of us interested in transforming, or at least influencing, our established political institutions. One perspective, which has by no means yet gained either widespread popular approval or general elite acceptance, suggests that the immediate urgency of dealing with environmental imperatives will require the resort to more authoritarian forms of government.[1] The solutions which emerge from this "radical" perspective usually endorse the principles of elitist management to a much greater extent than has been considered appropriate in the past decade. This can be seen most strikingly in the work of Paul Ehrlich, Garrett Hardin, Robert Heilbroner, William Ophuls, and Dennis Pirages.[2] The position of ecologically concerned economists and public policy analysts, though certainly less apocalyptic and less directly authoritarian than the forementioned, often implicitly sanctions the resort to more elite control because of the contention that these issues are fundamentally technical concerns to be solved within the burgeoning field of environmental management.[3]

This chapter maintains that these perspectives misunderstand some crucial parameters of the contemporary crisis of affluence and ignore the emancipatory potential within the ecological censure of liberal-capitalist and state-socialist polities. The eco-critics have described with acumen the deleterious consequences of liberal-capitalism's development. But after outlining all the faults and incapacities of our current modes of political organization, the eco-critics' call for an end to liberalism ironically terminates by recycling the solution of the most distasteful liberal, Thomas Hobbes, in the guise of tragic realism. This not only exhibits a singular lack of imagination but probably also contains an unrealistic estimation of the political capacity of most advanced industrialized nations. Although the espousal of elitist management carries fewer complications and more parsimony than the advocacy of democratic-participatory movements, the former solution is often less effective and less realistic in actual practice. I will examine three areas in which the advocacy of elitist management falters. My initial focus is on their uncritical and generally misguided discussion of class, ideology, and ecological politics. I then move to question the contention that environmental science necessarily entails a diminution of our commitment to democracy. Finally, I address the connection between scarcity and theories of human nature in order to note that the political remedies of the eco-critics are not solely based on a scientific estimation of objective economic conditions, but are thoroughly intertwined with explicit and implicit ideas about human nature—ideas whose validity is open to serious doubt.

One final prefatory statement needs to be made. It is not always a simple chore to trace the important elements of the argument advanced by many political ecologists. Most students of politics who came to the study of environmental issues brought with them liberal-democratic values and, in the case of Heilbroner, a lifelong commitment to democratic socialism. This occasionally results in hopeless confusion as an author still professing a commitment to democracy endorses a decidedly authoritarian government. At the very least, these authors feel compelled to issue statements testifying that the conclusions reached are advanced with the utmost reluctance and are antithetical to the personal values which the author has previously cherished. At the risk of erecting and jousting with a straw man, my argument will largely ignore these protestations and disclaimers. Such remarks are obviously honest and perhaps tortured statements made in the Weberian tradition of social science, but it is not the authors' good intentions and democratic sympathies that I question. For better or worse, and I think for the latter, these theorists allow their personal desires and predispositions to be overwhelmed by the "scientific" evidence that they offer as proof for their political stance.

Environmental Science and Class Politics: Boarding the Spaceship

The metaphors we employ in our political analysis betray what we deem important; they shape, to a large extent, the solutions we present. If we think, as some scholars did in the sixties, that politics is best conceived as analogous to a physical system, we will be attentive to questions of equilibrium and system persistence but likely ignore dilemmas of social change and discontinuity. Because metaphors serve this exclusionary function, they ought to illuminate and not distort. When our metaphors are distorted, the political analysis which follows is apt to be incorrect. This is especially germane in the case of political ecology.

A fundamental premise of political ecology is that we are all in the same boat, or better put, the same spaceship. This metaphor implies that certain extinction is our common fate (or at least our grandchildrens' fate) if we don't manage to modify the behaviors which have environmental deterioration as an indirect consequence. Admittedly, this spaceship metaphor houses an element of truth, but it simultaneously obscures the origins of ecological dilemmas and the political context in which they should be placed. The spaceship metaphor can lead us to think that ecological issues constitute a recent nexus of problems, issues specific to advanced industrialized societies. And it would be obviously incorrect to support this presumption. Ecological dilemmas impinged on the politics of the preindustrial world, and even today, we can see environmental dilemmas which do not have their source in industrialization. Such examples as the Kansas dust bowl and perennial soil erosion and flood problems come to mind here.[4] Nor were ecological problems absent at the inception of the industrial revolution. Bentham was attuned to these dangers, and reformers thereafter have been periodically concerned with the miserable environmental conditions of the workplace.[5] What we see today is nothing uniquely "modern," "post-modern," or "post-industrial" but is what Hans Magnus Enzensberger has incisively described as the "universalization" of a perennial condition.[6] The politics of ecology is one more example of an issue not placed on our political agenda until it has become evident that the children of the wealthy are not immune and have contracted the disease. It is heroin come to the suburbs.

To be sure, the realization that heroin use affects the children of the affluent or that we see environmental imbalances everywhere does not diminish the seriousness of the problem. Problems should not be dismissed as unreal when the upper middle-classes complain. We should, however, be wary of making shared problems the principal indicator of a common situation. Other things may not be so equal. It remains legitimate to ask the question which Enzensberger has posed about environmental legislation which purports to improve the quality of life: just whose life is going to be made more beautiful, and at whose expense?[7] A single-minded focus on environmental scarcity tends to overlook other scarcities which have contributed to the degradation of the human community, e.g., scarcities of compassion, scarcities of equality, and scarcities of ordinary activities which are both meaningful and environmentally sound. The manner in which political ecologists employ the spaceship metaphor overlooks our relative positions on the vehicle by lumping together those who are riding first class with the rabble huddled in the engine room. The lack of attention most ecologists show to class politics will be a practical liability, because a necessary component of any ecological politics that hopes to obtain widespread support must be a greater equalization of class differences.

Recent events tend to uphold this contention. We are beginning to witness mounting opposition to any formulation of our ecological dilemmas that ignores such a standard political issue as unemployment. European socialists have always been uneasy about the ultimate direction of political ecology, and American laborites have become increasingly willing to accept a measure of pollution and environmental deterioration if existing employment opportunities can be maintained and new ones established. The curtailment of economic growth recommended by ecologists is occasionally said to be antithetical to the goal of full employment sought by laborites and their sympathizers.[8] Moreover, a number of union leaders and workers see in the ecology movement a potential threat to the privileges that they as workers have gained through arduous and sometimes bloody struggle. They believe that they are now being asked to give up these privileges voluntarily or have them taken away, either through direct government intervention or by the impersonal coerciveness of the market.

This confrontation is seen most clearly in the limits on personal consumption which ecologists advocate. The union member knows that his automobile costs more because of the required installation of antipollution devices, and he is aware that he frequently pays more at the gas pump because his car travels fewer miles per gallon than a similar model did ten years ago. He also knows that the cost of antipollution equipment in his factory and other factories will ultimately be passed on to him in the form of higher prices. The worker is directly affected by the impact that reducing environmental danger may have on the availability of consumption benefits, and this concern is not really addressed by our current work in political ecology. We cannot pretend that the gripes of labor are somehow unreal or unconnected to the "genuine" problem because personal consumption benefits—whether we consider them to be legitimate human aspirations or artificial needs imposed by a capitalist economy—have been to a large extent the principal offering of American industry to its workers.

Political ecologists must address the question of how we can create and maintain employment opportunities, create an ecologically sound workplace, and offer laborers something more worthwhile than a stream of increments in their consumer benefits. This is not only or principally a question of how we can adjust members of labor unions to environmental imperatives but one that could well be linked with the historical leftist quest to socialize the means of production. Enzensberger has offered the ingenious observation that the universalization of ecological problems, contrary to what some ecologists are fond of asserting, need not be said to refute the Marxian analysis of capitalist development; instead, this may corroborate Marx's worst fear that capitalism, if not transformed into socialism, would eventually degenerate into barbarism.[9] In the recent past, the political activity of both American union leaders and most European democratic-socialists has been directed toward obtaining a bigger slice of the economic pie for their working-class constituencies. The less tangible, but perhaps equally important, goals of altering the nature of the work experience and reducing alienation have been frequently sacrificed in exchange for an increase in more tangible wage benefits. This view is also reflected in our conventional methodologies for studying politics. Politics is said to be the study of "who gets what, when, and how"; little mention is made of the quality of human relationships which occur during these distributional proceedings. Ecological imperatives may foreclose the possibility of activists and scholars continuing to adhere to these strategies. But to suggest that workers should be removed from participation in the consumer society without concurrently supporting and working for the realization of an economy organized according to more humane principles only constitutes an addendum to our history of blaming the victim. It is important to understand and to act with an awareness that environmental issues are not unrelated to the "halfway" manner in which we have tried to resolve the political dilemmas of advanced industrial societies. Ecological worries are, in part, an outcome of fueling the growth economy—whether it be organized along liberal-capitalist or state-socialist lines—without altering the inequalities present in the nature of human relationships.

The spaceship metaphor becomes even more unsuitable when environmental dilemmas are placed within a comparative international perspective. Once again, the issues outlined by political ecologists undoubtedly exist, but in a more complicated and ambiguous form than they describe. Who was not taken aback by the recent disclosure that radioactive fallout from a Chinese nuclear test passed over the U.S., and who is not more than a bit disturbed with the knowledge that carcinogens infiltrate our bodies from pesticides sprayed on Asian and European farmlands? And the number of oil spills from ships who register under a foreign flag in order to avoid complying with our safety standards can only be described as an outrage which demands an immediate remedy. Furthermore, the standard analysis of political ecology relates these isolated events to a theory of global environmental deterioration. Ecologists forecast in elaborate detail the grave dangers that the interrelated incidents of sustained population growth, resource depletion, and increasing pollution may unleash on the entire world. The objection to the aptness of the metaphor is similar to that leveled against it in the context of domestic politics. Simply put, the lack of resources and the possible catastrophe predicted for the future by some political ecologists also happens to describe, with uncanny accuracy, the actual life of nearly half of the world's population at this very moment.[10] The international class-stratification system currently existing serves to make governments of the Third World wary of accepting any proposal put forth by advanced industrial nations to limit Third World industrial and agricultural expansion. Third World governments—especially if a sizable proportion of their population is underfed and if the average male dies at forty-six—find it difficult to consider seriously the request that they refrain from the utilization of pesticides that may induce cancer in the adults of industrialized states.

A similar controversy has been repeatedly provoked surrounding the issue of reducing population growth. Population problems are extraordinarily complex and cannot be explained by either facile Marxist reasoning or by a simple denunciation of the peasantry for their proclivity to multiply. Population is, at times, a problem of too many peasants, but it is also a political outcome of gross inequality within nonindustrialized societies and the profligate use of resources within the relatively affluent nations. In this respect, one commentator has suggested that Western nations ought not to expect nonindustrialized societies to conform to our demographic theories while our economic and political theories consign these nations to a subordinate position.[11] This is not to say that the relatively affluent nations have either the duty or the capability to establish a system of worldwide equality immediately, but that a genuine recognition of an interdependent world will call for a greater moral and practical sensitivity to the political questions of international equity. The first principle of political ecology states that "everything is connected to everything else"; certainly this is overstated, nevertheless, it is of critical importance that ecologists recognize the necessary link between social questions of equity and scientific predictions of scarcity.[12]

Some political ecologists have, of course, remained sensitive to the international class dimensions of an impending ecological crisis. Robert Heilbroner's scenario of potential worldwide destruction emerges from his speculations about the political consequences of the redistributive demands that relatively nonindustrialized nations will likely make on the states of the industrial world once they attain the capacity to deliver nuclear weapons. Heilbroner offers a profoundly chilling analysis, but his entire enterprise is slightly tainted from the outset. His fault is not that he struggles with complex issues only to reach an unpleasant conclusion (reasons for objecting to the particulars of his analysis will be discussed below), but that the sort of predictive-theoretical work in which he engages misconstrues the appropriate function of the social theorist in the contemporary age. Insofar as Heilbroner and those who do similar work have informed us of the complexity of ecological problems, publicized and sensitized us to the global interdependence of person upon person, and issued warnings about the possible catastrophic effects of nuclear class-war, they have furnished us with a valuable analysis which could serve as an incentive to action. But insofar as their analysis terminates with either predictions of doom or thinly veiled urgings to submit to an authoritarian leader, they exhibit a paralysis of imagination which serves the cause of fatalism because the practical consequence is a paralysis of positive action. The task of social and political theory extends beyond this exercise of our predictive faculties to the more demanding chore that we keep alive the idea of a world in which the primary values include more than mere survival.

The necessity of this task can be clearly established if we examine the political probability of which Heilbroner writes. The political likelihood of a nuclear class-war, as Heilboner admits, is not equal to the probability that Ted Kennedy will retain his seat in Congress the next time he campaigns for re-election. Heilbroner's worst scenario is more akin to Marx's prediction that the socialist revolution would unseat the capitalists from their positions of hegemony. Akin, not because of any political affinity, but because the realization of the scenario is predicated upon an abrupt departure from previous actions and not upon a simple extension of previous behavior patterns. Moreover, these predictions can be "refuted" by conscious human intervention directed toward a contrary goal. To implement the socialist revolution required both that laborers attain more than a trade-union level of consciousness and that capitalists not utilize the tools at their disposal to defer it. The same is true about the possibility of nuclear class-war. It implies an actual willingness on the part of Third World nations to employ tactical nuclear weapons and an inclination on the part of the superpowers to allow this to occur. Seen in this perspective, it is quite likely that the stronger nations will intervene at some time before this becomes a realistic threat. The critical issue is the precise nature of the intervention. The problem is that the politics of survival justifies almost any intervention, no matter how inhumane it is. Without the motivation and constraint that conceptions such as fairness and equity engender, we inhabit a world in which the paramount value of survival is itself continually threatened by our inability to imagine anything else.

The final weakness evident in the ecological discussion of class politics becomes apparent if we begin to question the tactical realism of a solution which advocates an increased dosage of coercive management. If questions of equity and freedom are ignored, from where are we going to recruit this ecologically minded elite? Just how realistic is the election of an ecologically directed leader and through what institutions will this unselfish elitist pass? Is it realistic to think that we shall soon witness a leader emerge from a statehouse or Congress with widespread popular support, ready to proclaim and enforce stringent environmental regulations without a more positive program?[13] I don't think that political ecologists are speaking about the possible election of Jerry Brown or Mo Udall—politicians currently in the system generally sympathetic to environmental concerns, for neither could truthfully be considered the revolutionary that political ecologists deem necessary. Nor are they thinking of President Carter's plan concerning the redirection of our energy efforts. Why then, the question remains, does coercive management still appear to be the only possible answer to our condition?

This tendency in political ecology is a consequence of the analysis of liberalism that is offered. Ecologists suggest that the economic tenets of liberalism are grounded in a philosophy inappropriate for our era and that the standard liberal methods for reaching public decisions are inadequate to the task of environmental regulation. The assessment of societal well-being in terms of whether or not our macro-economic indicators are increasing leads to an ultimately destructive commitment to the growth economy. Equally distressing is the political fact that interest-group liberalism contains no rational method for assessing priorities and acting upon these. "Lowi's evaluation concludes that interest-group liberalism has come to a dead end because it is an ineffective means of governing. However, Lowi was poorly acquainted with pressing environmental issues when he wrote. If interest-group liberalism fails on so many counts to meet today's needs, it will fail even more miserably to meet the needs of the future."[14] To argue that it would be beneficial to move beyond interest-group liberalism is fine, but to leave the criticism at that or just to present us with a laundry list of maneuvers (take money out of politics, revise the seniority and committee system in Congress, control the political influence of large corporations, etc.) is really no help at all.

Liberalism, even in its interest-group variety, is more complex than the analysis of the ecologists indicates. Are not there some interests which are legitimate and should not these legitimate interests be furthered? One chore involved in moving beyond interest-group liberalism is to separate those interests which deserve to be advanced from those which do not. (Should health-care lobbies, for instance, be banished from our legislative corridors?) This is no simple task but it is one that the ecological critique of liberalism has yet to consider. Furthermore, are not there positive elements in the liberal tradition which ought to be expanded? We know that interest-group liberalism has not worked successfully and may never work to deal with ecological issues in a satisfactory manner. This recognition does not, by itself, tell us in which direction we ought to move. Can we today accurately say that further democratization (at the workplace and in communities) which expands and concretizes the formal participatory tendencies of liberalism will not help to alleviate the causes of environmental deterioration? Can we say that coercive management will? Political ecologists have not grappled with this issue in a convincing fashion. They have not done so because the critique of interest-group liberalism is really only a veneer that covers, but does not quite disguise, their utter disenchantment with the practical activity of politics itself.

Environmental Science and Democratic
Competence: Re-ending Ideology

There is a clichéd image depicting the relationship between the scientist and the politician that few of us would uphold these days. This is a picture that one might see in a grade-B movie. The scientist—garbed in white, toiling in his lab—is oblivious to the activity of public men. The gruff politician remains equally distant from the affairs of the scientific community because of his commitment to the practical, sometimes petty, affairs of the everyday world. We find a number of problems with this image—both in its inaccuracy in depicting the actual relationship between the two spheres, and in its implications about what the proper relationship should be. We know that—despite the reluctance of some modern governments to formulate a comprehensive science policy—there is an undeniable connection between the scientist and the politician and that questions concerning the relationship cannot be ignored. To determine the proper relationship, however, is a task of considerable magnitude which has confounded and beguiled our most astute minds.

One answer which has periodically appeared is the formation of an alliance between the members of the political establishment and the scientific community. The alliance relationship is characterized by a reciprocity in which both partners work toward a common goal. In this respect, we think of government funding of cancer research in an effort to rid industrial America of a prominent killer. The scientist and the politician each utilize his particular forte—the former his scientific training and the politician his ability to divert funds from the public treasury for research facilities—to work for the shared cause of preventing death from the intake of carcinogens. The alliance may also be ongoing without a public affirmation of its existence. We might think here of the Manhattan Project in which scientists labored to achieve the military goal of creating a weapon capable of abruptly ending World War II.

Another simple formulation is the notion that it is the duty of the scientist to serve the politician. The starkest manifestation of this conception is found in the practice of totalitarian science in which the validity of scientific theories is contingent upon the receipt of the party's imprimatur. More subtly, we might think of the dictates of scientific value relativism which underlie much of modern social science: values are decided through the political process, and the scientist provides the politician with the instrumental knowledge necessary to reach the desired goal.[15] We might point to Operation Camelot in which the U.S. government hired social scientists to develop methods of counter-insurgency which could be applied against Latin American revolutionaries. The day-to-day manifestation of this relationship in political life is usually much less devious. It takes the form of Alan Greenspan heading Nixon's Council of Economic Advisors or people from Brookings joining Carter's advisory team. At times, the scientist also serves the politician in a manner which is not so overt. Thus, a specific political figure may employ the scientist merely to legitimize a decision by investing it with the aura of expertise.

Politics has often, however, adopted an adversary stance vis-a-vis science, and the converse also frequently occurs. I am thinking of Chairman Mao's statement that it is better to be "red than expert" and the periodic Chinese efforts to implement economic growth by "exertion of the will." In a somewhat dissimilar vein, Richard Nixon expressed his conception of the tension between science and politics when he told a group of future scientists that, as president, he could assure them that "there is no political science." Here Nixon was asserting his belief that politics is a pragmatic activity which cannot be either completely understood or effectively practiced according to the dictates of science.

Scientists themselves have frequently opposed our political leaders. Today, the opposition takes the form of protesting governmental or political intrusion into the peer-group review process. It is also evidenced in the repeated controversies about whether governmental dictates should be permitted to stifle the pursuit of advanced research on the grounds of potential human danger. Scientists may also oppose this or that particular government policy which has no bearing on the direction of their own future research. Scientists who opposed both their colleagues and the government in the matter of dropping the bomb come to mind in this regard. So do contemporary scientists who publish the risks involved in a potential leak from a nuclear plant. Technocrats may also express opposition to the actual practice of politics through the methods of silent infiltration. They undermine the nature of the political without explicitly stating their opposition to it. I am thinking here of the increasing bureaucratization and technicalization of government that has occurred seemingly in the nature of things. This is not only the case of hiring more bureaucrats and experts, but something much more extensive; politicians themselves seem to become bureaucrats by explaining their reasons for political action in the technical idiom of efficiency and bureaucratic competence.

These last musings allow us to realize that the opposition of science to politics may be more profound and deeper than a contrary perspective held on this or that government policy, especially if we define science both to include more than a set of procedures invented in the seventeenth century and to embrace the classical idea of what Paul Kress has noted to be "disciplined and systematic inquiry."[16] This opposition takes the shape of a scientific disgust with the entire process of politics. This objection finds the gap between the demonstrated truth of science and the direction of our political affairs to be unjustified and intolerable. So Plato creates his Republic to replace the corrupt Athenian democracy which has sentenced the wisest man in the city to death and suffered defeat in war because of the lack of individual devotion to the common interest. Hobbes' distress at the affairs of seventeenth-century England led him to formulate his inexorable science of politics which might render continued political activity on the part of the citizenry unnecessary. Sheldon Wolin has noted that the extent of Hobbes' animus toward everyday political affairs was such that he refused to impose the Platonic requirement that power be wedded to knowledge and virtue.[17] Survival was sufficient in his nasty cosmos.

This perspective on the relation of science to politics is shared by a number of political ecologists. Resorting to a class analysis, which would call them middle-class, fails to capture the intrinsic element of their work. Politics for them is a luxury which in the complex world that we inhabit today must be sacrificed to the knowledge of science. Environmental science, their analysis implies, must be accorded precedence over our long-established modes of public decison-making in order to ensure survival. Like those of Plato and Hobbes, the recommendations of political ecologists exhibit a profound uneasiness with the very idea of politics because of its purported incapacity to discover genuine truth. The concerns and opinions of the average citizen are simply misdirected and not properly attuned to the objective reality of scarcity.

Enzensberger, it was noted above, referred to the centrality of the spaceship metaphor because of his contention that it serves the ideological function of obscuring class divisions within industrial societies. Equally important is the corollary of the metaphor's second assumption about the relation of politics to science. Not only are we all cruising in the same vehicle, but only a few of us are competent to be at the controls. Witness the statement of Paul Ehrlich and Dennis Pirages concerning the profession of politics. "Long range planning in a very complex society will require a much higher level of competence in politics. Governing must be reserved for wise and dedicated individuals rather than being allowed to remain an arena where representatives of vested interest fight to retain their disproportionate share of rewards. There will be little room for mistakes in coordinating the affairs of a densely populated and highly interdependent society, if that society is to survive future challenges."[18] William Ophuls has presented a similar line of argument concerning the political incompetence of the average citizen in these matters. "Thus, the closer you are to a situation of a vessel embarked on a dangerous voyage, the greater the rationale for the rule of the competent few. But as the earth and its various territories approach more and more closely to a realization of the spaceship metaphor with each step toward the ultimate ecological limits, the highest degree of competence will become indispensable for effective rule: and even a democratic theorist might have to echo Plato's *Republic;* the polity is a ship of state that must be commanded by the best pilots or it will founder."[19] The politics of environmental science which begins with a critique of interest-group liberalism finally becomes a critique of democratic politics per se. The bargaining and compromise that characterize politics can be ill afforded on the spaceship. Politics must be restrained. Like schoolchildren who bicker on the bus ride to class in the morning, we will, at best, only hurt ourselves; at worst, we may also distract the driver and cause all of us to overturn. The prudent man who can grasp the complexities of scientific forecasting must also be capable of controlling the squabblers.

In the context of American politics, this retreat from democratic measures by political ecologists is sadly ironic because it was the critical, participatory ethos of the sixties which brought the majority of ecological principles into public consciousness. Despite its theoretical weaknesses, strategic blunders, and practical excesses characteristic of American radical movements, the politics of the sixties achieved a number of significant advances. The notion that we should and could encourage more widespread participation in our political culture was of particular importance. Demands were couched in a new language that spoke of power to the people, community control, and political involvement. It was this new language and the new activism that it helped to engender which informed citizens that they could act collectively to combat discrimination, to stop private industry from polluting the air, and to halt state bureaucracies from running highways through our neighborhood.[20] In the sixties, the idea of democratic competence was infused with a practical and effective richness rarely seen in our political history. This permitted the environmental movement to escape the suffocating boundaries of the conservation movement and to become enmeshed with a political analysis that espoused organized citizen-action as the antidote to public decision-making by private concerns.

This historical perspective on participatory theory and practice in American society is not incidental to the analysis. We should remember that proposals for popular control in the sixties developed in concrete opposition to the claims of the so-called end of ideology school. This thesis informed us that the fundamental problems of industrial societies had been solved and that the solutions to the few anomalies which remained were technical and apolitical. For example, the more ardent proponents suggested that the economy was doing quite well and only in need of "fine tuning." The majority of us were urged not to bother with political activity but rather to enjoy the activities on the yacht in which we were cruising. Rather than get involved with the boring chore of manning the controls, we were implored to permit those minds fascinated with the intricacies of mechanical calibration to indulge unobstructed in their hobby. The argument wasn't convincing to many of us. We believed that some of the anomalies were best characterized as systemic problems of poverty and discrimination. We also felt that relying primarily on the good will of the technocrats was not the best method for bringing these issues into public consciousness and for bringing these problems to a satisfactory resolution.

Political ecologists have revived the end of ideology thesis but in an opposite form. Whereas it once postulated that our fundamental dilemmas had been successfully resolved, it now warns us that the boat on which we blithely sailed is today in immediate danger of sinking. But if we look at the sixties (as political historians may someday do) to be an era not of failures but of tentative beginnings and significant ideas incompletely realized, the burden rests with political ecologists to prove why we should assent to their notions about democratic imcompetence and elite capability in the politics of the future.[21] A number of reservations come to mind which should support our reluctance to accept the conclusions posited in this regard. The first reason, as discussed above, is the continuing relevance of class divisions in industrial societies. The second reason is the imprecise nature of ecological predictions. The final reason addresses the misguided notion, which pervades their recommendations, of what political competence means.

I need not rehearse the controversy which has raged within the scientific and professional community since the predictions of early doomsters were issued. Sufficient to note here that predictions of imminent or even inevitable ecological catastrophe are not thought to be completely accurate by all members of the scientific community.[22] The more important fact is that if ecological disaster arrives, it will emerge in human and not merely technical terms. The political configuration within particular nations and among the nations of the world will likely determine the precise form of ecological catastrophe. For example, the predicted world food shortage, expected to be intensified by the large increase in the world's population in the next thirty-five years, will not occur simply due to the technical issue of having an insufficient supply of food to feed the number of people existing. The political dilemma of inequality in the consumption and distribution of food will be a decisive determinant of what form, if any, this crisis will assume. And once it is admitted that equity matters constitute a principal component of environmental crises, attributing decision-making competence only to a particular cluster of people becomes unwarranted.

The terms of crisis and eco-disaster which are employed by political ecologists can also be an obstacle to clearheaded analysis. Whereas their warnings are purported to be based on accurate scientific predictions, they can only furnish the most minimal details to describe the precise nature of the impending crisis.[23] But by speaking the idiom of crisis, they conjure up images of previous struggles: the worldwide economic collapse in the thirties, political systems faced with the threat of invasion and war, and societies in which any semblance of dignity and compassion has been discarded in favor of sheer animal terrorism in a war of all against all. Each is an image of an event in which consent to strong and relatively unfettered leadership appears to be the proper response. One does not have to go so far as to echo the simplistic belief that World War I was fought merely to make the world safe for the vested interests to note that in times of previous crisis one of the cruelest tragedies has been the manner in which the risks were assigned. So that even if genuine threat does exist in our present case, we should be wary of assuming that political elites by themselves are best capable of distributing risk. Also, it is crucial that talk of future crises not obscure the range of human choice that still remains available.

The notion of "competence" held by political ecologists is open to serious question. Political competence, for them, signifies both the desire and the ability to control the natural and political environment in a manner which is not ecologically harmful. Their version carries strong elitist overtones; it is envisioned as an individual capacity found only among political leaders. This conception of what political competence entails is unduly narrow. In broadest terms, political competence simply denotes the ability to get along well in our collective lives—something we should wish the entire citizenry to develop. It means being free of unwanted domination whether by the elements, by machines, by the organizations we have created, or by other human beings. Beyond this, political competence means being capable of making reasoned decisions in conjunction with other people, and of being cognizant of our dependence upon others. This is not at all the same as bureaucratic efficiency because it demands the inherently social ability to interact with others. Metaphorically speaking, it means to be at home and not to feel like an exile or a stranger in relation to the world we inhabit.

No doubt, there is a crisis of political competence in our age, but it can not be thoroughly grasped if we characterize it as a paucity of technically sophisticated and ecologically aware political leaders. A better historical analysis would regard our "political incompetence" to have its roots embedded not merely in the technical complexity of our age but in a pervasive ideology of elitist democracy which has considered us to be political adolescents and has, in effect, scripted the outcome. Just recall how Richard Nixon described us in an interview that was released shortly after his re-election. We are, he said, like children in a sense that we are capable of assuming some political responsibility but rapidly overwhelmed by it all if we are given too much to shoulder. Let me not be misinterpreted here. More participatory variants of democracy are not grounded in a philosophy which attests to the scientific and technical proficiency of the average citizen; indeed, these suggest that citizens should delegate to scientists control of those matters over which they are competent to judge. Participatory variants of democracy, however, preserve for ourselves (with input and discussion from scientists) the significant decisions concerning the direction of our lives.

If one believes that ecological issues are, in the final tally, political issues or questions about how we should organize our collective lives, the expertise of the scientist cannot become the sole criterion for decision-making. This is not to deny the importance of scientific warnings, but rather to argue that our political situation is more complex and perhaps more precarious than these can possibly contain. We need to muster all our capabilities and all our collective energies, and utilize our political imagination in ways that require more than a competent leader in a position of political management. Science becomes, in this view, a source of information and a form of persuasion, not a method of coercion. Scientists introduce ecological issues into public discourse and offer what they consider to be plausible solutions. But this does not establish an entailment relationship. Environmental science by itself can detail no particular manner of organizing our lives. There can be no single formula of political relationships that can be definitively connected to an environmental imperative.

The argument disputing the supposed need for more coercive management has so far turned on a number of points. I have suggested that ecological issues cannot be accurately described as technical problems and have noted that elite management has a notorious and not particularly efficient history in our polity. It might also be added that it was popular movements which brought ecological issues into public consciousness in the first place and organized citizen action which has achieved much of the limited success which the ecology movement has garnered. There is another reason for the advocacy of less management that is not contained within the conceptual and strategic considerations mentioned above, though this rationale is less easily grasped and less easily justified. This is to state the belief that more participatory modes of existence not only aid us in developing our capacities as persons but can be a significant constituent of living in accord with ecological principles. This contention is best explained by contrasting it to the description of human nature which is either articulated or implied in the standard ecological analyses.

Environmental Science and Human Nature: The Obedient Self

Ecologists frequently criticize what they consider to be the mistaken notions underlying liberal theory which have led nations to follow a twisted set of priorities. William Ophuls has suggested that the tenets of Lockean liberalism can only be upheld if Locke's assumption that "all the world is America" is accurate. Lacking material abundance and living in a world of resource scarcity, Ophuls has maintained that we may have no other choice than to embrace Leviathan. But this reading of liberal theory and what ails it is profoundly incomplete. Ophuls is correct to rehearse the usual commentary on Locke's thought in order to note that Locke's revision of Hobbes was based to some extent on his divergent idea concerning the quantity of resources available to the industrious person. Yet this was not necessarily the key element in Locke's revision nor is it reason enough to make us believe that excessive material abundance is a precondition of our freedom. Scarcity and abundance are frequently relative concepts, and we can surely discard the idea that goods are unlimited without necessarily embracing the austere solution of Hobbes.

More pointedly, the case for the necessity of more authoritarian control by our governors rests not only on an estimation of our resource capability but also on an implicit model of man. Hobbes did not write the first thirteen chapters of *Leviathan* for no reason whatsoever. He described a psychology of human behavior in meticulous detail in order to persuade his audience that rational people could do no better than accept the government which he proposed. He hoped that his potentially authoritarian solution would be decidedly more enticing (and certainly more reasonable) than the chaos they were experiencing.[24] Moreover, although he could not bring himself to deny the sovereign full authority whenever a political decision was needed, he clearly believed that in most instances people could continue to live their lives while the sovereign took care of political matters.

Political ecologists often speak the language of Hobbes in modern form. Whereas Hobbes felt that the sovereign would leave us alone in most instances, the ecologists speak of macro-constraints and micro-freedoms. They talk of small self-sufficient communities within an authoritarian structure. But merely echoing the language of Hobbes doesn't permit them to escape the criticisms that have been leveled at him. Certainly Hobbes did attempt to make a division between macro-constraints and micro-freedoms. One reason we find him unpalatable is that we're not certain that he actually succeeded. The simplest objection always raised is that Hobbes provided us no guarantees against an excessively harsh ruler. Another objection to the Hobbesian resolution is distinct from the question of protection. We don't consent to Hobbes' argument because we know that much of the personal is political. Our particular desires, hopes, fears, and the general manner in which we live are connected to our social and political mores. And it is because of this inevitable connection that we are distrustful of tidy divisions. The same holds true for the ecologists' macro-constraints and micro-freedoms argument. Despite their good intentions here, the argument is often a piece of intellectual sleight-of-hand because a number of their suggested alterations have nothing to do with maintaining micro-freedoms. For example, "the only way we can preserve and cherish other and more precious freedoms is by relinquishing the freedom to breed and that very soon."[25] But what is the freedom to breed if not a micro-freedom? The freedoms which may have to be subsumed under macro-constraints may well encompass the principal freedoms which advanced industrial societies currently grant its citizens.

The necessity for the removal of these freedoms is justified by presenting a model of man and a subsequent notion of rationality that is borrowed from Hobbes. Obedience, it appears, can be rationally enforced in no other manner. Ecologists describe this over and again by reference to the tragedy of the commons. The story is one of a common pasture which is being increasingly overgrazed. This predicament cannot be easily resolved because it is not rational for each herdsman to decide on his own not to add another animal to his flock each time such a choice becomes a genuine opportunity. "But this is a choice reached by each and every rational herdsman sharing a commons. Therein is the tragedy. Each man is locked into a system that compels him to increase his own herd without limit, in a world that is limited. Ruin is the destination toward which all men rush, each pursuing his own best interest in a society that believes in the freedom of the commons. Freedom in the commons brings ruin to all."[26] Rationality, according to Hardin and others who agree with him, is equivalent to a self-interested market evaluation of personal utility.

Hardin's dilemma is fundamentally the problem of how to obtain an approximation of the public interest in a market society that is populated by individuals who do not publicly acknowledge and act upon their connection to one another. The most frequent answer to this enigma has been to establish a system of coercive laws that will confine the pursuit of self-interest to a limited sphere and will permit the government to referee any dispute that might ensue. The government exists to rectify the weaknesses, the greed, and the lack of substantive rationality in ordinary men. Other answers, however preferable these may be, are defined to be unreal. "Real altruism and genuine concern for posterity may not be entirely absent but they are not present in sufficient quantities to avoid tragedy. Ony a Hobbesian sovereign can deal with this claim effectively. We are left with determining the concrete shape of Leviathan."[27] Obedience is irrational unless each individual is assured that everyone else will be forced to make the same sacrifices.

In a sense, this is a compelling argument. Why should one middle-class family do without two cars when all their neighbors continue to keep their garage fully stocked? And why should one person, for other than personal financial reasons, lower the temperature in his house if he believes that most others will still keep their thermostat at a comfortable seventy-two degrees? Individual restraint in these situations appears futile and naive. One manner of conceptualizing these dilemmas, however, doesn't have the advocacy of a Hobbesian sovereign for its logical conclusion. Such an approach might take more seriously than political ecologists themselves the criticism that they make of market liberalism. Ecologists note correctly that it has been liberal market governments which have encouraged the desire for individual material aggrandizement. Yet they omit from their analysis the critical fact that Hobbes himself is not exempt from this charge; his psychology describes market man, and his political theory takes this notion of rationality for granted. The return to Hobbes and more coercive authority (assuming the enormous strategic barriers mentioned above could be hurdled) is nothing more than a return to our basic problem. Unless we insist that we acknowledge in a theoretical and practical manner our connection to one another, it will remain impossible to develop alternatives to personal consumption benefits as the epitome of a worthy standard of life. The bind we find ourselves in today is one consequence of the very retreat to the micro-freedoms so well advertised in market societies.

Robert Heilbroner reaches a similar conclusion about the necessity for obedience to an authoritarian leader but has little confidence that this can be implemented in a rational manner. His concern is not to describe the self-defeating implications of "rational" behavior in a market society but to discover the irrational sources that may lead us to submit to the dictates of national authority. Heilbroner describes what he believes to be the psychological component of the iron law of oligarchy. Because his views amount to a refutation of my previous argument concerning the possible realism of an authoritarian solution, I will follow his argument closely.

> If the boldest and most far reaching exercise of political power will be unavoidable over the future, this does more than introduce a random element about which nothing can be said. It raises the question of whether this exercise of power will be successful, in the sense that it will be accepted by those over whom the power will have to be exercised. One cannot have political power without political obedience, one cannot have strong government without a sense of national identification. How do we know that the use of power which emerges as such a central necessity for the survival of mankind will in fact be accepted? What can we say about this? Here fortunately we are not quite in the dark. For the behavioral traits which permit the use of political power lie within our scrutiny, even to a certain extent within our predictive capabilities.[28]

Heilbroner locates this trait in the first few years of our childhood experience. Political authority provides a "sense of psychological security by recreating the accustomed relationships of sub- and superordination to which our long period of helpless dependency has accustomed us."[29] This dependency becomes translated into a "perplexing readiness, even eagerness, with which authority is accepted by the vast majority. An acquiescence in, or search for, a hierarchical ordering includes not only the lower and middle reaches but also the upper levels of society."[30] And this readiness and willingness to give consent to charismatic leaders lend wide discretion to the sort of political structures that might be formed. Whatever structure is instituted, however, will have to include strict authoritarian controls. "Revolutionary regimes will be able to perpetuate extreme egalitarian structures only through a succession of leaders endowed with tremendous authority, or else move in the direction of reestablishing the legitimacy of violations of authority that are now regarded as violations of the revolutionary spirit."[31] He then defends his argument in a curious fashion by endowing it with the mantle of inevitability and subjecting anyone who may disagree to an ad hominem slashing. "Nonetheless, it would be foolish as well as hypocritical, not to admit that tendencies toward authoritarian rule seem to be a chronic feature of political life; how many egalitarian revolutions have not ended in the creation of a political establishment every bit as authoritarian as that which it originally displaced? It behooves us to understand this 'logic' of political behavior as well as possible, particularly in view of the extraordinary difficulties with which democratic governments will be faced in the coming decades and generations."[32]

I don't profess to be adequately trained to provide a detailed analysis of Heilbroner's discussion of childhood and its subsequent meaning for political behavior. I am more than a bit uneasy with it. My own inclination would lead me to depict this period in a more complex framework which emphasized not only the acceptance of authority, but also the simultaneous rebellion against it.

I think I am on somewhat firmer ground to dispute Heilbroner's logic of political behavior to which he believes we would be foolish not to agree. Certainly revolutions have been betrayed and our noblest hopes dashed, though not always in the manner he describes. Some betrayals had their source in persons who were never so interested in equality in the first place. But to leave the logic of political behavior with Heilbroner's comment is exceedingly disturbing. To deny the authoritarian tendencies of our politics is foolish, but to filter out of the analysis our profound tendencies toward democracy and self-rule is equally preposterous. Have not movements of democratic dissent frequently arisen just when hierarchy, excessive order, and bureaucratic stifling seemed to have overwhelmed our collective spirit? There is no 'logic' of political behavior that drives us to establish unbridled authority just as there is no logic that inevitably moves us toward directly democratic methods of governing. The genuinely sad part of Heilbroner's logic is that he becomes an unwitting accomplice to it and an apologist for its implications. The ecology movement which had its beginnings in the cultural-democratic politics of the sixties and which had most of its limited successes because of organized citizen action, acquires its rigid authoritarian overtones through the type of book Heilbroner writes.

The final element of Heilbroner's analysis attempts to explain our readiness to consent to authoritarian leaders on the national level. Like a child who divides his world into his own extended family and those outside it, so do people divide their world into those within the national borders and those outside. "For this manifestation of the political element in human nature makes it utopian to hope that we will face the global challenge of the future as an international brotherhood of men. . . . It is unlikely in the extreme that mankind will enjoy a setting in which the indentifactory potential within 'human nature' can be extended to embrace men and women of other peoples or that considerations of a pan humanistic kind will displace the narrowly familistic basis on which identification is today founded."[33] Our incapacity to connect our interest with an evaluation of the rights of others outside our national borders does have a positive implication. "It is important to recognize that nationalism despite its potentially vicious application, is not solely a destructive force and that political identification with all its problems is by no means only a dangerous element in human nature. I am inclined to believe that it is the saving element in human nature."[34] Heilbroner thus assays to bestow the calculating and detached Hobbesian sovereign with the emotional devotion granted to Filmer's ruler. The state, according to this explanation, functions as a surrogate father and because of our intimate relation to it, we become willing to undertake chores and make sacrifices that are inappropriate when viewed from outside the confines of familial ties.

This is not the place to commence with a detailed elaboration of competing psychoanalytic theories in opposition to Heilbroner's. I do want to mention some misgivings I have with Heilbroner's conception and briefly describe an alternative conception of the self that might be more relevant to our environmental dilemmas. I'm not convinced by Heilbroner's presentation that we are by nature obedient creatures who strive to realize an innate desire by assenting to the demands of political authority. The history of rebellion against authority is simply not explained in this depiction. Nor does this assertion recognize the delegitimization of traditional authorities which has occurred during the past decade. Finally, I am not certain that obtaining personal fulfillment through vicarious identification with entities such as the nation-state manages to lead us in an ecologically viable direction. If we do have a complex of states in which the citizenry is permanently worked up to a feverish pitch, the danger of war, as Heilbroner admits, is excessive. It is also not clear that resorting to a succession of authoritarian rulers could necessarily help ecological matters because this depends on the political bent of the ruler with whom we are identifying. Alone, the notion of the obedient self is mute in regard to what daily activities could substitute for those pursuits which are deemed ecologically harmful. The moments of vicarious identification are usually limited, and the notion of the obedient self just may not impart meaning to the everyday lives of most citizens.

To a belief in man as the obedient soul, we might fruitfully contrast the idea that we are inherently social beings. This suggests that we develop our full capacities only through sustaining interactions with others, and that we can get the nourishment for complete human development from no other source. Without these, we become diminished selves who lead half-lives. Through genuine social relationships, the satisfaction of physical desires and the performance of mundane tasks assume a significance that is not intrinsically contained in the action. Marx described this quite beautifully in the *Early Manuscripts* when he wrote of how social relationships could enrich and transform the life of egoistic man by elevating his "animal" needs and desires to the status of truly human needs. In this regard, the satisfaction of our sex drives becomes both an expression of our capacity to give and a recognition of our need for intimacy; our work with others becomes an acknowledgement of our dependence on them and connection to them while we create a common world. Heilbroner's obedient activity is an impoverished substitute for genuine symbolic interaction that comes from relations with significant others and active participation in a common life.

This social conception of human nature harbors different political implications than those lodged within the notion of the obedient self. Primarily, the social self calls for the encouragement of more participatory and public modes of existence. We would move less in the direction of coercing obedience to predefined goals and more toward opening channels of participation that have been previously blocked at the workplace and in our localities. The implication is not that participation will immediately and automatically serve the cause of ecological security but that it is the best method of public education. The belief is that only through conversation with others and participation in common decisions do we begin to recognize and to acknowledge through action the legitimate wishes of others. Nor is it implied that workplace and local democracy will enable us to ignore stark questions of power and issues of national importance. But these issues are best dealt with through a system of truly public representation in which our mediators are more than political brokers; this is a system which private people who are merely obedient cannot possibly establish.

But this is all very abstract and somewhat removed from concrete ecological issues. It is fine to talk about the educational possibilities of increased participation but what, the reader might ask, is to be done about tangible environmental dilemmas? What is the theory that will allow us to defer environmental catastrophe? Well, it probably can be said that these issues won't be resolved in a theory which only envisions its task to be that of predicting future events based on extensions of present trends. Theories of this ilk lead to fatalism or to a false sense of security by offering a technical solution that purports to manage the problem. The worth of a theory that we urgently need will not be found only in its formal elegance or predictive capacity but in the impetus to human transformation that it contains. And though I don't pretend to be capable of fulfilling this need, I think it may be of some use to perform the more modest task of connecting the strands of the argument presented throughout the essay in my concluding remarks.

The first conclusion is that political ecologists will have to connect their prescriptions to our current unresolved economic and political issues. They will have to explore in greater detail the possible connection between the ecological belief in the need for a labor-intensive economy and the standard liberal goal of putting everyone who wants to work on the job. Ecologists also have to address the issues of providing economic security to all and establishing more participatory modes of work. This is not only for the tactical purpose of gaining a wider political base but because of the possible relevance that the transformation of our economic lives may have for our ecological dilemmas.

The belief needs to be asserted—and it is only a belief that can be proven or disproven through political action—that a political arrangement with a greater degree of economic fairness, equality, security, and participation may well lessen our commitment to a high consumption society. This is the utopian meaning of socialist economic goals: our lives qua economic men become a matter of fact for everyone and not a matter which becomes the source of our ambitions, struggles, and anxieties. The interpretation of the ecological crisis offered here contends that this goal not only possesses enduring relevance but that it is actually more important than ever. This is also the precondition for a system of public representation that can transcend the brokerage function that our representatives now perform.

It would be incorrect to assume that ecological contradictions can be resolved solely within the realm of political economy. The positive message of the ecology movement lies not in its critique of the inability of liberal capitalism or state socialism to cope with ecological distress but in the movement's intimations of the meaningful human advantages we can create and, in turn, receive by living an ecologically viable life. Certainly some emotions and beliefs can be tapped in this regard if we can possibly imagine more creative methods of political and social action. There is an increasing tendency to denigrate the human consequences of the consumption economy. Scholars write about the boredom and anxiety produced by it. Popular songs deny its advertised magical powers, and public opinion polls have shown the lack of purpose that our citizens feel in their lives. Although the precise alternative to a high consumption society cannot be explicitly detailed as yet, we do know that it would call for the enrichment of our public life and the enlivening of what Richard Sennett has called "our dead public space." The ecology movement should emphasize not only the denials that will of necessity occur, but the value of engaging in life-affirming activities that are ultimately more worthwhile than partaking of market pleasures.

This is not to deny that we are involved in a race against time. It is to say that there is no certainty or reasonable probability of resolving ecological dilemmas without settling the unresolved questions of class and without reconstituting a strong measure of public life. It may well be a race against time. But if I have to run for my life, I would rather not do it with a stick prodding me or with others passing me in their cadillacs, or with a motivating psychology which allows the person behind me to step on me if I fail. I would rather do it with friends at my side to encourage me when I falter and minister to me when I stumble. It's the only way to travel.

Chapter 7

Frail Hopes

I attended a lecture a few years ago at which a social scientist was explaining his theory about the proper and most humane way to organize the economy and the government. He had recently published a book that had gained some professional acclaim for its novelty, and as he lectured to a combined group of faculty and graduate students, I perceived that he considered himself to be something of a prophet who was spreading wisdom to those of us who were unfortunately wedded to outdated perspectives on social or administrative change—be these the conventional pluralist analysis of political science or the established radicalism of the Marxist variety. At best, he was a minor prophet because his audience was unlikely ever to extend beyond his professional compeers, and his ideas were unlikely to gain an effective and intelligent constituency.

I recall how I was put off with the pretentiousness of the entire presentation and how it offended my decidedly ironical sensibilities about the importance of academic work. But this distaste was really secondary to the anger which welled up in response to what I considered the blatant irresponsibility of his analysis. After the speech, a good portion of the audience queried him as to the strategic omissions of his theory. They wanted to know how we might begin to organize the economy and the government in accord with his desires. They wanted to know what concrete steps could be taken next week, next month, next year. Our speaker dismissed the relevance of these inquiries with a casualness that was profoundly disturbing. I was not annoyed because he could not provide a detailed blueprint of his proposed alterations. Few of us can trace a futuristic political architecture without skimping on the fine details. But I was aggravated to learn that he felt the question was simply irrelevant, that he would suggest that these banal strategic considerations would be neatly resolved in the near future. We would have, he claimed, the choice of organizing society in the manner he described or of perishing from the consequences of ecological imbalance. It was quite a cavalier posture to assume. It was as if he was eagerly awaiting the arrival of environmental catastrophe so that he might discover whether his thesis would be confirmed or disproved. He simply ignored the obvious fact that there is more than one possible response to ecological dilemmas short of catastrophe and that all these responses have far-reaching human implications that need to be discussed and evaluated. I was not excited by his prophecy but was even less impressed by his lack of ambiguity concerning the choices we make in the organization of human affairs.

The task neglected by our speaker of combining general theory with strategic recommendations that will help us to cope with a wide range of connected dilemmas is one that surely imposes an exceptional strain on our imaginative capacities. While I can think of a much more preferable condition than our present state, it is an ideal that I can only express in the broadest of terms. I, as others, would like to be a citizen of a nation that can pursue the ideals of economic equality without a strict reliance on consumption pursuits, and I would want to help create a society in which we could live meaningful worklives, participate in significant political decisions, and partake of a vibrant social life. But what precisely does this mean for those of us who write about politics and those who are politically involved on other levels? What relevance should these desires have for the ordering of our everyday political lives? Though I believe in the practical significance of these queries, I have no answers which I definitely believe are correct and no vision which could be implemented tomorrow in order to transform our approximation of the welfare state into a society which fulfills the human needs and acknowledges the environmental imperatives denied today.

I began this book by asking whether the most vibrant type of liberal reformism currently existing could ever be capable of meeting what I consider the essential needs of the time. I answered in the negative. While admitting that Nader has presented a significant critique of contemporary American society, I ultimately contended that his politics are not the most appropriate model for progressives to follow. In a series of essays explaining Nader's purpose and ideology, three principal arguments were advanced to support this position. I argued in Chapter Two that Nader's challenge to the American corporate structure has not adequately addressed the reigning class divisions in American society and that his campaigns against the misuse of technological expertise has not been sufficiently sensitive to the threat that technological reasoning might eclipse moral judgments altogether. Chapter Three suggested that Nader's defensive liberalism implicitly accepts the conventional wisdom that our lives as consumers should be the standard by which the quality of life is determined. He thus ignores the hidden victimizations caused by identifying the good life with the consuming life and is unable to foster the cooperative, communitarian politics which he endorses. Finally, in Chapter Four I suggested that his attachment to the consumption ethic noticeably weakened his capacity to propose imaginative responses to our environmental threats.

Nader's weaknesses in this regard are understandable insofar as American liberal reformism has rarely adequately responded to conditions in which resources are perceived to be limited. In the face of this weakness, it has been a constant temptation for people on the Left to advocate the establishment of strict authoritarian governments when resources are admittedly finite in order to temper the excesses of democratic-capitalist nations. After examining the arguments of Thorstein Veblen and some contemporary political ecologists, I concluded that the rejection of a democratic participatory politics is unwarranted for a couple of reasons. The pragmatic argument that authoritarian governments are necessarily superior to democratic governments in the potential treatment of these issues is still unproven.[1] An even more important shortcoming in the authoritarian argument is evident once we come to understand that more democratic, more egalitarian, more public forms of organization may provide an attractive and significant alternative to the high consumption, privatized life-style that has been one source of reckless resource consumption.

A reader might suggest that my tendency to criticize Naderite liberalism from a leftist perspective is inappropriate when one considers the constraints under which liberals now operate in the American political arena. American liberals, it might be argued, are constantly threatened by much stronger conservative opposition than is found in most other industrialized democracies. The consequence is that liberals have been driven to stake out positions which can be introduced to the population without generating the charge of "radical" from more conservative elements. The liberal dilemma is especially noticeable in 1979 because the business community has become decidedly more aggressive in it political commitments and because of the increasing popular skepticism which imperils initiatives which propose ample use of the government's power. Listening to American political rhetoric in 1979, the average person is likely to hear conservatives decry twenty years of expanding government, twenty years of excessive limits on government spending, and twenty years of creeping socialism (as opposed, of course, to "marching" socialism). Is not it asking too much for liberals to do more than guard themselves on their conservative flank?

Perhaps not. My blockheadedness in this matter has the following rationale. Anyone who has read his Louis Hartz knows that American liberals have infrequently challenged the fundamental requisites of corporate capitalism. Typical liberal programs such as social welfare programs, income maintenance proposals, and entire wars on poverty have not been predicated on a fundamental redirection of economic priorities and a redistribution of both wealth and income. Yet despite the liberals' reluctance to endorse these methods of political action (a reluctance only occasionally born from expediency, more often stemming from an ideological congruence with conservatives and a genuine desire to distance themselves from others on the Left), conservatives have never been known to congratulate liberals for their sweet reasonableness. To the contrary, liberals are routinely denounced as flaming socialists intent on dismantling the free enterprise system. Yet if my argument that one failure of American liberalism has been its unwillingness to question the standard economic wisdom is thought sensible, we see that liberals are placed in the bind of being labeled radical without making any actual moves in that direction. The sad result is that one important response to our condition is described as unworkable when it has never really been seriously considered.

An equally important problem with the belief that a holding pattern is the best posture for a liberal to assume these days is that it can also prevent the necessary self-examination that recent events should force upon progressive activists. By picturing themselves as political monks engaged in a valiant and lonely battle to preserve the eternal verities from extinction, liberals often fail to note that their own variety of politics— even if permitted full expression—could not successfully meet the challenges with which we are confronted. The position underlying this work is that troubled times for the Left should generate more self-criticism than smug complacency. To renew a progressive dedication to a better sociity requires not only a denunciation of current trends, however justified this may be, but also an honest recognition of how reform movements themselves are implicated in the persistence of undesirable public habits and institutional priorities. The times require as much vision as pragmatism, as much innovation as willingness to "hang tough," and as much self-examination as dedication to traditional principles. I want to finish this book by explaining why a modified democratic socialist politics may be relevant to our current dilemmas and by describing the significance of more participatory solutions to our current dilemmas.

The Losses of Pragmatism

I have contended throughout this work that American progressive reformism in its Naderite dress has been reluctant to criticize certain controversial issues because of an implicit calculation of political expedience. This calculation of expedience or escape from difficult choice-making has been most glaringly evident in Nader's propensity to ground the public interest in the preferences that he attributes to us as consumers. While Nader's critiques have been pointed to the extent that he believes that consumption should be safe and protected, not completely unrestricted, Nader has also assumed that human beings are primarily consumers of goods and services. So despite his vehement opposition to American business and his recent notion that capitalist decision-making should be revised along the lines of consumers' democracy, Nader has been unable to speak of the "public interest" without frequently reducing it to the desires, often selfish desires, that we share as consumers of goods and services.

At the inception of Nader's activism, this conceptual problem was not mentioned by many people as especially significant. By describing the extent to which the practice of "business as usual" negatively affected our health and safety, Nader issued an important warning to members of the American middle-class who had viewed the affluent society through roseate lenses. I am sure that many activists and thinkers on the Left believed that the value of the warning exceeded the problems caused by Nader's failure to understand the profound human alienation which pervaded consumer societies. Yet as the resource limits on consumption activity become evident, the undesirability of defining ourselves as consumers is now compounded by the realization that this might also be practicably impossible. But so long as the debate about Nader remains determined by the standard liberal-conservative terminology—i.e., is he a reformer working in the public interest or an elitist telling us what to eat, drink and wear—the importance of discovering human activities that are both nonalienating and environmentally sound remains a secondary consideration.

Nader's habitual reduction of the public interest to safe consumption is unfortunate because he is by no means an obtuse liberal. He is capable of learning about new issues, and he is sensitive to environmental concerns and matters of occupational health and safety. Unfortunately, Nader has not understood or, if he has understood, has not acted on the contradictory pulls in his analyses. Instead of concentrating on the need to speak about restraints on excessive consumption desires, Nader has become a contortionist who twists himself and the intellectual underpinnings of consumerism to the limits of plausibility. When conflicts arise between the contrary pulls of his analyses. Nader is apt to claim that there is no tension and flail at the special interests. Listen to him attempt to argue that there is no conflict between the environment and jobs. "Congress should pass legislation requiring the environmental protection agency to investigate every threatened or proposed plant closing involving twenty-five or more workers if it has reason to believe that the cost of environmental controls is the reason. Another law should require companies laying off employees due to environmental controls to pay workers' wages for six months after their dismissal."[2] Nader's commentary is valuable insofar as it recommends limitations on the chicanery occasionally practiced under the mantle of environmental costliness, but it is nonetheless far removed from questioning the worth of our devotion to consumption and many of the products routinely marketed by the private sector.

Deciding upon the proper response to environmental threats has become an irritating and ever-present enigma for those who have considered themselves to be liberals or further to the Left on the American political spectrum; indeed, the perplexity is shared by many of a leftist persuasion throughout the world. We have seen that a number of writers who profess to be imbued with liberal and socialist values have recanted their commitment to democratic norms and suggested that without the establishment of a coercive government, people will rarely act in accord with the commonweal. Robert Heilbroner tells us that we can only survive by discarding the pleasurable amenities of everyday life and doing without the luxury of democratic politics. But what have we left after Heilbroner removes the political liberties and the consumer choices that are the essential components of the welfare state? Nothing but a mystificatory and opaque state that uses its powers to exact obedience from the citizenry. Heilbroner and other reluctant authoritarians reduce in age from the adolescents who populate liberal theory—capable of some participation if mediated through representative structures—to children who have yet to perceive the foibles, the weaknesses, and the living humanity of their parents. We are to become child-patriots in love with an abstract state and engaged in fighting a war on the environment and perhaps other more bloody struggles as well. We shall march to the tune of "my daddy can beat your daddy up." Liberal theory offered us the formal right to participate and to be partially responsible for our ultimate fate. Now these mechanisms are said to be inoperative, and we are to obey orders without being guaranteed the right to participate in their formulation. But we like to do it anyway, according to the rationalization; obedience is in our nature.

This shift to more authoritarian beliefs by writers who at one time espoused progressive values is illustrative of a principal flaw in a liberal reformism that considers us to be primarily consumers of goods and services. By painting ourselves diminished and incomplete, we eventually paint ourselves into a corner from which we are unable to flee. Once reduced to a package of pleasures and pains, whenever the progress is slowed and the growth halted, we become victimized by our very own self-definitions. The consequence of this reduction of human nature is that in the hands of some of our scholars and activists (and unfortunately in some of our lives also) the reduction becomes a self-fulfilling prophecy. How else can a pack of atomistic pleasure-seekers and pain-avoiders be constrained other than by the enlightened promulgation of restrictions on personal liberty?

There is a sad irony to all this. In the past, measures that dealt with common, public needs rather than the mere aggregation of private ones had to be left outside the purview of our political concerns. Those who proposed that politicians move further leftward—by devising platforms and campaigns that would acknowledge the complete range of our social needs and desires—were ridiculed by the devotees of realpolitik and denigrated by others for possessing an irrepressible will to lose. This scorn seems to have been misplaced today because these clever practitioners of the fine art of the possible now make severe ecological imbalances and political strife seem a possible and perhaps imminent threat. Those who refused to acknowledge that people need public space to talk about common matters, those who refused to imagine that politics could be the shared accomplishments of responsible people, those who simply envisioned government to be the beneficent provider which allows consumers to choose their private pleasures from the multiplicity of available consumer goods, and those who did not ask fundamental questions about our priorities and values lest they be considered elitist, all now stand bereft of imagination and creative political will in the face of events.

It is also possible that liberal reformers, in the name of pragmatism and expedience, have come to accept the definition of our wants and needs that has been promoted by the corporate elites even when this description could have been challenged. Perhaps a politics of material self-interest was never desired with the intensity that we have come to associate with the pursuit of self-interest. In a fascinating study of the economic growth controversy in contemporary French politics, Volkmar Lauber has maintained that the wishes of the underlying population have been vastly divergent from the interests of political elites concerning the wisdom of unchecked economic advance. He argues that while elites, including communists and socialists, have consistently supported economic growth policies, the public has not been equally approving.

In order to defend his contention, Lauber cites a number of French public opinion surveys in which citizens were asked their preferences concerning the rate and direction of economic growth. The results, he argues, are surprising to people who think that the pursuit of material self-interest is the mechanism animating the political behavior of the citizenry. Blue-collar workers in France believe that the production of individual consumer goods should be curtailed in favor of more extensive investment in and development of public goods. They also testify to a belief that rapid industrial development is accompanied by widespread personal unhappiness. Lauber also suggests that France might not be an aberrant case and that similar opinions might be found in all the major industrialized nations, including perhaps the United States. He concurs with an assessment that American public opinion is too mixed to say assuredly whether it supports the decision of many politicians to subordinate environmental matters to a host of other considerations.[3]

I would be reluctant to suggest here that these surveys indicate the general population might endorse a politics of public goods and relational needs to replace a politics of material self-interest. Equally, I would be reluctant to accept survey data contrary to Lauber's as incontrovertible proof that an alternative politics could never be created. Questions of economic growth, personal desires, and attitudes toward the environment are extraordinarily complex and laden with assumptions and implications not easily delineated in the confines of a questionnaire. We might be strongly against economic growth but such a question, standing alone, is an acontextual one. What if my reply has a bearing on whether I will keep my job, on whether my brother in Florida will keep his, or on whether somebody in Missouri with whom I am not acquainted will keep his or hers. I might be willing to endorse a slight decrease in my standard of living, but only on the condition that David Rockefeller's standard of living also drops significantly. We obviously need to have a complete accounting of what alternatives are available before we can assume that answers about economic growth given on a doorstep will translate into concrete political action of a particular bent.

The intriguing thought generated by Lauber's research is to wonder whether we could possibly politicize issues that have previously remained off our political agenda. He implies that if given a choice between economic growth and expansion of leisure-time activity, the majority might opt for leisure. Because of this possibility, Lauber avers that traditional liberal political theory with its emphasis on private enjoyments might still provide the appropriate theoretical underpinnings for an environmentally viable world. Two major problems inhere in this formulation. The first is that he ignores the routinization of leisure according to capitalistic norms that has occurred in most advanced industrialized democracies, especially the United States. Secondly, even if the possibility that a society devoted to leisure was environmentally sound, it may not be an especially praiseworthy community, for it does seem that we might only be enslaving ourselves to the soma of a brave new world. If the citizenry—and this is certainly yet to be determined conclusively in American society—holds a substantial animus toward the malevolent consequences of economic expansion, could we possibly create a society in which the practice of politics denotes a loftier activity than the management of the corporate economy? Assuming that this could possibly be the case, it might be worthwhile to speculate about the substance of a politics directed at this end. My belief is that a politics of different expectations which progressives might advocate should be presented as a modification of traditional democratic-socialist goals, looked at sensibly in the light of changing ecological and resource conditions.

A Politics of Different Expectations

Much of the literature which speaks about environmental reasonableness assumes that orthodox perspectives on politics are incapable of solving ecological dilemmas. A reader is likely to digest statements maintaining that we have to go beyond the Left and the Right, that we have to establish authoritarian governments, that we have to create a "Buddhist politics," that we have to build a city of man founded on the tenets of planetary humanism, and that terms such as capitalism, liberalism and socialism are irrelevant to our present condition. It is as if the ecological crisis can only be solved by creating a new term adequate to its management. I have concurred with this assumption insofar as I have asserted that a reformist politics which considers us to be primarily consumers of goods and services will not be able to speak persuasively of the common good. But it is not at all clear that a modification of traditional democratic-socialist politics will be as irrelevant to the cause of environmental reasonableness as the previous comments imply.

I intend to flesh this argument out by referring to an article written a decade ago by Michael Walzer concerning the proper stance for democratic socialists to adopt in a liberal capitalist society. In his piece "Politics in the Welfare State," Walzer advanced four principal claims. 1) Liberal politics since World War II has resulted in more humane policy outcomes than previously. 2) The benefits of the welfare state have unfortunately been accompanied by costs which democratic-socialists necessarily deplore. 3) Despite these human costs, democratic socialists really have no choice but to work for the perfection of the welfare state. 4) When the perfection of the welfare state appears to be in reach, progressive activists should then pursue a strategy of "hollowing out the state." Below, I will briefly present Walzer's justification for each of these points and suggest that a reconceptualization of his perspective will still allow democratic socialists to have something important to say about the direction of American politics.

1) Walzer began his article by acknowledging the significance of the welfare state measures that had been recently established. "The fight over welfare is important enough given the immediate economic demands of the poor themselves; given the sheer rapaciousness of the rich and the powerful, the fight for some minimal standards of distributive justice takes on all the moral significance that has been attributed to it in a century and a half."[4]

2) He then expressed a deep ambivalence about these achievements by calling attention to the negative underside of the welfare state. "The problem of the welfare state is that the public recognition of needs, our hard won visibility becomes another source of social control. . . . Welfare administrators function, whether consciously or not as double agents; serving the minimal needs of the individual and upholding at the same time the social system that is being invaded."[5] This unwitting service is performed by almost all the agents within the organization. For instance, doctors provide needed medical care to the infirm but also reinforce trends toward the professionalization of health care; well-intentioned schoolteachers often help to reproduce the prevailing socio-economic structure. The client, on the other hand, exchanges good behavior for a measure of private happiness.[6]

A second problem with the welfare state is that it basically ignores the realm of experience outside the family and the household. "One of the ways that liberal states promote happiness is by encouraging men to stay home. Hence the crucial principles of welfare distribution are first—that benefits ought to be distributed to individuals and second, that they ought to be designed to enhance private worlds."[7] Walzer recognized that to remove the possibility of public life was to make a distressingly reductive evaluation of human beings. Yes, there are private needs and wants that we desire to satisfy, but we also have relational desires and social needs that the liberal platforms never seem to contain. "Politics is something more than welfare production. It is a vital and exciting world of work and struggle; of aspiration, initiative, intrigue and argument; of conscious effort, mutual recognition and amour social; of organized hostility, of public and social achievement, of personal triumph and failure. The welfare state offers no satisfactory substitute for any of these."[8] Indeed, the perfected welfare state, with only a smattering of public men, turns us into a society of hospital patients because it "involves the surrender of everyone's say in the determination of future restrictions (or expansions), a surrender of any popular role in determining the shape or substance, the day-to-day quality of our common lives."[9]

3) Walzer suggested that his indictment of the welfare state and the strategies of liberal political activists should not serve to minimize the importance of maintaining the alliance between all those who considered themselves on the progressive Left. To emphasize the ultimate differences in belief was irrelevant to most of the battles at hand, and Walzer believed that this would be the case for "sometime, probably the foreseeable future." Democratic socialists need to walk hand-in-hand with liberals, even if the former view their ultimate destination with grim sobriety.

4) When the benefits of the welfare state are firmly in their grasp, democratic socialists would need to be politically reborn and turn to the chore of "hollowing out the state." "What socialism requires is not that the welfare state be surpassed or transcended, whatever that would mean, but that it be held tightly to its own limits, drained of whatever superfluous moral content and unnecessary political power it has usurped, reduced as far as possible to an administrative shell within which smaller groups can grow and prosper. The state is not going to wither away, it must be hollowed out."[10] On the national level, this process means that we prevent the government from using its powers to involve the populace in adventures that only meet the interests of the leaders. On the community level, this means that citizens should take control of education, culture production, and community planning. "This requires a different kind of politics, not the kind to which we are all accustomed aimed permanently at the state, but a politics of immediate self-government, a politics of relatively small groups."[11]

Each rereading of Walzer's article never fails to leave me as impressed as when I first encountered it. There is a nobility to his sentiments and an integrity to the ambiguity that he explains in his struggle with liberalism which is clearly present. He recognizes that the consequences of liberal politics often include public impotence, and he couples his appreciation of our economic needs with the awareness that the welfare state cannot possibly satisfy the rich diversity of human strivings. The article is the work of someone who knows and appreciates the possibilities and complexity of life well enough to see the potential nobility of politics even when it is garbed in the shabbiest of outfits. Walzer's participant is akin to Marx's social man, a person rich in needs and ambitions, cognizant that his full potential cannot be achieved in the comforting refuge of the home without sustaining reactions outside with significant others.

Walzer's proposal about the most advantageous strategy for American progressives to follow is understandable. The recommendation that the extension of welfare state services be pursued is an attractive minimalist strategy. Despite the political lethargy and excessive bureaucratization that accompany the creation of a welfare state, the goal is a solid, tangible achievement. If liberation is not achieved, some measure of dignity occasionally is. If capitalism is not overturned and the captains not removed from their position of influence, at least they are reminded that we are watching and are no longer willing to attribute the accumulation of their largesse to an innate or an acquired moral superiority. They will, at the very least, have to be effective schemers to translate our reforms into benefits that will accrue to them. We could sacrifice speaking about public happiness and social needs, but propose to attend to these later. Once again, would not any other tactic be considered impractical and unjustifiably sectarian according to the ordered consensus of American politics?

Today, however, I believe that democratic-socialists and other progressives need to rethink their position in respect to the continued expansion of the welfare state. The unarticulated but taken-for-granted premise of Walzer's analysis is that the full complement of welfare benefits can be extended to anyone who resides in an advanced industrialized democracy. The assumption derives from a belief held by many thinkers and activists that because capitalism has abolished scarcity, anyone who emphasizes the finite nature of the state's fiscal capacities is demonstrably not interested in poor people. While I am not attributing this specific belief to Walzer, his analysis does lend itself to this sort of interpretation. Consider, in this light, the proceedings of the Conference of Alternative State and Local Public Policies which met in Denver during the summer of 1977. According to a report, the Conference's primary purpose "is to provide a progressive, programmatic underpinning for state and local politics, to help activists and public officials view government at these levels as an instrument for social change."[12] Politicians such as Jerry Brown were denounced at the meetings for what was considered inexcusably callous behavior toward the poor.

> These decisions and similar ones taken by what they termed the "Junior Carters" in state capitals around the country were roundly denounced as a part of a growing neo-liberal theme of "lowered expectations." Democratic governors like Jerry Brown, Michael Dukakis, Ella Grasso and Hugh Carey were repeatedly attacked as moralists who invoke fiscal integrity as an excuse to trim on social programs, who cater to a tax beset middle-class by making scapegoats of the poor and the welfare system. They view concepts like lowered expectations and devices like government reorganization and zero based

budgeting as nothing more than machinations to buy time and put a little intellectual gloss on the copout. In public policy terms, what it all means is that those without jobs aren't going to get them and those who need decent housing and medical care can figure they're on their own. In terms of electability, it works. Says one of the conference leaders, 'poor people just don't sell well in America today.'[13]

This is the standard manner of conceptualizing our current situation. On one side, stand those who speak about lowered expectations; on the other, those who claim that such a politics is an excuse for allowing the economically disadvantaged to go unaided. Both positions are unsatisfactory. The politics of the lowered-expectations crowd is accurate to the extent that it is wrong to believe that the welfare state can or should be expanded indefinitely. But, Governor Brown's prediction that the poor will have to lower their standard of living would not be inevitable if restrictions were placed on the prerogatives of the wealthy. The flaw in the current exposition of a politics of lowered expectations is that it is so firmly embedded in the ideological substrata of our corporationist society. Change can only be initiated within parameters that are unduly narrow. Thus, we are presently witnessing the adaptation of ecological slogans to a capitalist society in which the invocation of nature is a technique for conducting class warfare.

Progressive activists are justified in their criticism of this tactic. But they are much less justified in acting as if their dismissal of the strategy warrants dismissal of the entire lowered-expectations slogan. We do need a politics of lowered expectations or, at the least, a politics of different expectations if the former phrase is repugnant. If the ecological crisis and our growing dependence on foreign resources is realistic and has political repercussions, one major consequence may be in the capacity of our society to provide an expanding array of welfare benefits. To be sure, this does not mean that the services we have commonly come to assume are the standard components of a civilized society will be eliminated, but only to say that we will have to determine carefully what benefits can be offered without exceeding what we presume to be our fiscal and ecological capacities. It also becomes incumbent on progressive activists that they not implicitly endorse a recklessly profligate existence on the part of the affluent as a quid pro quo for the extension of welfare benefits to the needy. Finally, it may become necessary to develop standards for the tradeoffs that will inevitably occur. Health care services are a good example. To put this issue in its bluntest form, we have now developed the capacity to prolong life and arrest the progress of certain diseases, but we may be unwilling to assume the economic burden that our scientific advances require. Certainly lives should not be extinguished or perpetuated according to the cost-benefit ratio of the illness contracted, but we still have to adopt a more sensible attitude regarding the human services that can be provided by the state. This entails discussion of standards, the making of hard, distasteful choices, and the substitution whenever possible of human for technological action.

But, *and it is a critically important "but,"* these choices can only be made legitimately after we have committed ourselves to more generous standards of distributive justice than those which we presently follow. A politics of lowered expectations may indeed be warranted, but it should only be implemented after we make the most reasonable and humane decisions about whose expectations are going to be lowered and why. Similarly, there is nothing unreasonable about the state articulating a commitment to the neediest members of the polity, but the commitment should be grounded in an argument that speaks about human dignity and distributive justice, not disguised as an altruistic method for distributing a surplus that is the result of unlimited abundance. A politics of different expectations should not imply that only the poor will sacrifice or that a commitment to the disadvantaged will be made solely at the expense of people occupying the rung above them on the economic ladder.

A commitment to more generous standards of material justice may also help to demystify the precise nature of our economic and ecological condition. In a situation where inequality is supposed to be pursued, distrust becomes an almost automatic and natural reaction to appeals which emphasize the necessity of sacrifice and frugality. "Why conserve?" the public asks. "The oil companies are only hoarding the oil to make greater profits later." To be sure, conspiracies of this sort have been unearthed in recent years, and so long as the conditions conducive to their formulation still exist, it will become that much more difficult for politicians like the President to persuade the public of the necessity to bear material hardships. The critical importance of realizing a better approximation of material equality when ecological imbalances appear to be threatening and when social trust is waning has been best summarized by Hugh Stretton. "Material equalities may not by themselves generate much brotherhood, but they are a necessary condition of it. They may soon be a condition of government by consent: the only workable basis left for social arrangements between political equals."[14]

At the moment, an intense devotion to fostering a much greater degree of material equality cannot be discerned in either of the two major American political parties. The current inattention to its relevance, however, should not lead us to bury the goal forever on shallow pragmatic grounds. Perhaps the most striking consequence of environmental issues is the manner in which issues formerly thought to be matters of purely personal preference have become included in the purview of public decision-making. Who would have thought five years ago that we would hear James Schlesinger today say that he did not consider the right to drive a car which traveled less than ten miles on a gallon of gas an essential and inalienable component of our political liberty? That we might come to see other even more controversial economic arrangements as matters of public debate is certainly not probable in the immediate future, but it is a frail hope not entirely foreclosed.

The Relevance of Public Life

Our beliefs about what should properly constitute political matters are frequently dependent on our perception and evaluation of events. Our reading of history and our definition of the significant issues that confront us will then color our notions regarding the proper sphere of political action. In fact, our more illuminating and innovative conceptions of the political are often borne from a profound disenchantment with the established state of affairs and the conventional wisdom about these. Historically, democrats regulated the power of the monarch by maintaining that political authority is not bestowed by the divinities. Tom Paine ingeniously requested that the colonists use "common sense" rather than conventional wisdom. Such is true also with contemporary theorists who have been concerned with what should be included under the name of politics. Hannah Arendt noted the lack of nobility and graceful civility of our politics, rebels against the perennial bickering over material interests, and rediscovers through her interpretation of the Greeks a purer form of politics that is untainted and uncomplicated by bargaining over economic interests. Paul Goodman, who believed that the bureaucratic and centralized state stifles the initiative of his fellow citizens, endorsed decentralization and community control of services. So what, he maintained, if a school district or two is run according to the tenets of the reactionary Birchites. Could things be that much worse than they are now?

A similar process of highlighting the relevance of what is noticeably absent can be discerned in our analysis of specific policy dilemmas. If ecological problems are described to be a consequence of a lack of vision and a failure of coordination in the planning process, a function of governmental inaction or a result of the inefficiency endemic to interest-group liberalism, the call becomes one for more centralization of government and stricter restraints on individual behavior. But if government centralization is held to be a prime determinant of ecological imbalances, the consequent recommendation is likely to emphasize decentralized structures, intermediate technologies, and perhaps even the relevance of anarchist politics. I have tried to suggest in this work that the most humane resolution of environmental dilemmas is dependent on creating a participatory politics that can both alter the priorities of American corporate enterprise and establish forms of public life that will enable us to escape the victimizations ignored by liberal reformism. In line with the idea of highlighting that which is notably absent, I have maintained (in agreement with others) that consumer societies neglect the social and public elements in our beings. Neither Naderite reformism nor environmental authoritarianism has recognized that we need opportunities to use our reasoned judgements to make the significant decisions which shape our lives in order to become fully mature, fully developed human beings.

To be sure, there are a few easy methods with which my belief can be denigrated. One practical taunt is simply to ask who has the time and energy to lead such an active political life. Merely consider the suburban commuter who spends three and a half hours each day going to and from work. Or does the laborer in a coal mine have the energy to engage in spirited political discussion three nights a week after spending much of his days in a draftless shaft? A skeptic might argue that even the public-spirited person of the participatory mythologists will soon be fatigued and overworked if he does not carefully budget his time. There are definite limits to what the conscientious citizen can do. Only so much reading can be done, so much time spent in political involvements, and only so many considered judgements can be rendered each week. We have other interests and other demands on our time that are both valuable and enjoyable. We spend time with our lovers, converse with our friends, and strive to meet new and interesting people. Perhaps, as Walzer himself once mused, to demand that everyone participate regularly in politics is an excessive request because leading a truly public life would take too many evenings.

Another tack which skeptics about more participation can take is to repeat the argument that political life is stifling and boring. Was Tommy d'Alesandro right for others as well as himself when he referred to politics as the process of consuming excrement each day? Just ponder all the seemingly trivial affairs that have become the subject of political deliberation. Students of politics have been careful of late not to draw a false distinction between matters political and matters administrative. They have astutely described the political content of numerous administrative decisions. So far so good. This criticism has enabled us to understand the administrative process and to regulate a few of its excesses. But what this politicization also means is that inherently noble and exciting items such as our water supply and sewage lines become eminently political and the main substance of our political deliberations. That few of us find discussion and action about these items rewarding is clearly a healthy response to the condition.

Finally, a critic might object that participatory answers are simply impractical given the technical complexity of contemporary politics and the necessity of a good measure of centralized decision-making. If one speaks with our proverbial skeptic about these matters, it is likely that he or she will be reminded of the difficulty of taking a defensible position on strategic arms limitation or on deciding how federal grant money should be allotted. These chores demand considerable expertise and men who must be, as Veblen put it, well-versed in cause-and-effect thinking. In this vein, I recall a campaign in which a candidate for a local board of aldermen ran on the platform that he would bring cost-benefit analysis to the board—certainly a man of which Veblen would be proud. We must admit, it has been said, that we live in a Hamiltonian age in which Jeffersonian idealism only constitutes a lack of commitment to facing realities.

In response to these objections, I can only advance some cautious and tentative rejoinders; nonetheless, I think these are serious qualifications and worthy of consideration, however tentative and problematic they may be. The objections of the skeptics who try to explain why we should not work to devise methods that will encourage more extensive participation make a case that is too pat and too wedded to our established methods of conducting politics. We can mistakenly reify procedures and structures that will be altered due to the force and magnitude of events—if not through our conscious and willed interventions. Fortunately, politics is a complicated process, and what can become political truths in the future are not always falsified by one, by one hundred, and sometimes by one thousand examples in the present. The objection concerning the lack of free time that we have in order to engage in politics ignores the evidence that many people do find the time to participate. Workers organize and strike, middle-class groups form public-interest lobbies, and poor people meet to discuss how their children might be given an adequate education. Nor should we forget that many significant decisions about our lives are not made after six p.m. Certainly we need not celebrate the obstacles to more widespread participation by enshrining them in a framework which attests to its impossibility.

Also, we need to consider our historical condition. If the ecological critics are correct in their assessment that we have reached the limits to consumer society, the relevance of political and public life becomes even more apparent. Our first concern is to think about the most appropriate methods for reaching the difficult decisions that a sober estimation of our material resources entails. Participatory decision-making is preferable because burdens are more easily and cheerfully assumed when they are democratically shared. Furthermore, the purpose of public life may be more helpful than is connoted in the practice of democratically choosing our restraints. Ideally, it will be through political action that we will choose to define ourselves as a community of citizens and sharers which determines its standard of living by the manner in which we interact with each other and not by the simple availability of consumer goods.

Now to speak about the potential excitement and nobility of public life first bespeaks a commitment to the removal of the economic, social, psychological, linguistic, and physical barriers that currently foreclose this as a genuine alternative. In mundane terms, this means that activists begin to consider seriously the redistribution of wealth, the manner in which the quiet desperation of consumer societies can be politicized, the planning of public space in cities and neighborhoods, the methods of implementing continuing education in everyday life, and the possibility of redirecting the attention of the media. In this way, we might begin to create neighborhoods, localities, and cities in which we can become proud of what we achieve and share in common. There will, of course, always be people unwilling to leave the felt comfort of their private abodes for the uncertain benefits to be gained from the company of others. We may, however, begin to create places sufficiently attractive to draw some of those disenchanted with the consumer life away from the gurus who currently spout destructive formulas for personal success and toward our effort to create a world that will support and enhance our common desire to become competent, moral, and fully mature human beings.

Notes

Chapter One. Introduction

1. This work focuses on Nader who is representative of the politics of contemporary public-interest liberalism. This exclusivity is not intended to slight
   other figures or minimize the differences among various public-interest
   groups, but to claim that the most vigorous strand of contemporary progressive political activism originated with Nader and that the best
   method of understanding it is to examine the features manifested in his
   actions. I also want to note that by calling public-interest action the
   most vigorous strand of contemporary liberal politics I do not mean to
   imply that it has succeeded in its self-described task of creating a politicized citizenry.
2. A sampling of the work written about Nader can be found in the following
   works: Charles McCarry, *Citizen Nader;* Thomas Whiteside, *The Investigation of Ralph Nader;* Ralph De Toledano, *Hit and Run;* Hays
   Gorey, *Nader and the Power of Everyman;* Robert Buckhorn, *Nader:
   The People's Lawyer;* David Sanford, *Me and Ralph;* Carl Auerbach,
   "Some Comments on Mr. Nader's View," pp. 503–08. Ralph K. Winter,
   "Economic Regulation vs. Competition," pp. 890–902.
3. This perspective can be discerned in: Robert Heilbroner, *An Inquiry into the
   Human Prospect;* William Ophuls, *Ecology and the Politics of Scarcity;*
   and Dennis Pirages and Paul Ehrlich, *Ark II.*
4. A crisis of affluence, as I employ the term, denotes a condition in which resources are not so scarce as to promote a situation in which only the
   "fittest" can survive or so plentiful as not to call for restrictions on personal and corporate use. It is a condition in which implementing the
   political belief that all citizens should be accorded a reasonable standard
   of material life will necessarily entail limiting the profligate utilization of
   resources.

Chapter Two. Public Interest Liberalism: A Sensible Alternative?

1. Charles McCarry, *Citizen Nader,* p. 183.
2. David Sanford, *Me and Ralph* is a good example of the anti-Nader work now
   surfacing in some popular forums.

3. James Fallows, Mark Green, David Zwick, eds., *Who Runs Congress?* intro-
    duction by Ralph Nader.
4. McCarry, p. 218–19.
5. Marti Mueller, "Nader: From Auto Safety to a Permanent Crusade, p. 981.
6. Mueller, p. 981.
7. Jack Newfield, "Nader's Raiders", p. 56. (Interviews with Nader.)
8. McCarry, p. 163.
9. Luther J. Carter, "Campaign G.M., p. 452.
10. "Meet Ralph Nader," p. 67.
11. McCarry, p. 114.
12. "Nader's Raiders," p. 491. Richard Armstrong, "The Passion That Rules
    Ralph Nader," p. 219.
13. Patrick Anderson, "Ralph Nader, Crusader," p. 106.
14. McCarry, pp. 198–99.
15. Newfield, p. 60.
16. "Nader's Neophytes," p. 27.
17. A sampling of the critical works on American pluralism would include: Peter
    Bachrach, *The Theory of Democratic Elitism;* Peter Bachrach and
    Morton S. Baratz, *Power and Poverty;* Henry S. Kariel, *The Decline
    of American Pluralism;* Henry S. Kariel, ed., *Frontiers of Democratic
    Theory;* William Connolly, ed., *The Bias of Pluralism;* Theodore S.
    Lowi, *The End of Liberalism;* Grant McConnell, *Private Power and
    American Democracy;* Rober J. Nisbet, *Twilight of Authority;*
    Robert Paul Wolff, *The Poverty of Liberalism;* Garry Wills, *Nixon
    Agonistes.*
18. Lowi, p. 72.
19. A minimalist solution to the problem might be to call for business to be socially
    responsible, while those with a socialist orientation would argue that
    such responsibility is impossible in a capitalist society.
20. Mark J. Green, *The Closed Enterprise System;* Ralph Nader and Mark J.
    Green, eds., *Corporate Power in America;* Ralph Nader, Mark J.
    Green, and Joel Seligman, *Taming the Giant Corporation.*
21. Murray Edelman, *The Symbolic Uses of Politics,* p. 4.
22. Clarke E. Cochran, "Political Science and the 'Public Interest,' " pp. 327–55.
23. The politics of writers who have spoken of the communitarian failing of lib-
    eralism vary widely and embrace both conservative and radical-
    democratic stands.
24. Daniel Boorstin, "Consumption Communities," *The Americans,* pp. 89–166.
A much better
    explanation of this period, stressing the socio-economic functions of
    consumption is Stuart Ewen, *Captains of Consciousness.*
25. Langdon Winner, *Autonomous Technology* p. 262.
26. Winner, p. 227.
27. Winner, p. 332; Jurgen Habermas, *Toward a Rational Society;* Herbert
    Marcuse, *One Dimensional Man.*

28. *St. Louis Post-Dispatch,* 16 March, 1978, p. 1B.
29. A favorable reference to the politics of the sixties will be made in more than one instance. These should not be interpreted as a wholesale endorsement of all that occurred but as a reminder that significant issues were raised which we ignore at our peril in our current effort to forget the era.
30. John S. Nelson explains this idea quite persuasively in "Toltechs, Aztechs and the Art of the Possible," p. 116.

Chapter Three. Defensive Liberalism and Nader's Grim World

1. Sheldon Wolin, *Politics and Vision,* p. 293.
2. Part of the discussion of the various liberalisms is adapted from C.B. Mac-Pherson, *The Life and Times of Liberal Democracy.*
3. Frances Fox Piven and Richard Cloward, *Regulating the Poor;* Bruce Miroff, *Pragmatic Illusions;* Murray Edelman, *The Symbolic Uses of Politics.*
4. Ralph Nader, *Unsafe At Any Speed.*
5. Ralph Nader, "The Infernal, Eternal, Internal Combustion Engine," p. 8.
6. Ralph Nader, "Inventions and Their Uses," pp. 32–34.
7. Ralph Nader, "Business Crime," p. 7.
8. John Chamberlain, "Auto Safety," p. 343.
9. Ralph Nader, "Watch That Hamburger," p. 15.
10. Ralph Nader, "Don't Eat That Dog," pp. 12–13.
11. Ralph Nader, "We're Still in the Jungle," p. 11.
12. Ralph Nader, "Something Fishy," p. 20.
13. Ralph Nader, "The Burned Children," p. 20.
14. The tragic irony of this situation was the recent discovery that flame retardant material may cause cancer.
15. Ralph Nader, "The Violence of Omission," p. 19.
16. Ralph Nader and Jerome Gordon, "Safety on the Job," p. 24.
17. Nader and Gordon, p. 24.
18. Nader and Gordon, p. 24.
19. John Abbotts and Ralph Nader, *The Menace of Atomic Energy.* Nader's commentary on the Pennsylvania radiation leaks echoes the concerns that he has expressed for a number of years.
20. Ralph Nader, "Making Congress Work," p. 19, and "Ralph Nader Takes on Congress as well as Big Business," pp. 388–90.
21. Susan Gross, "The Nader Network," p. 9.
22. Susan Gross, p. 8.
23. Ralph Nader, *Public Citizen Newsletter,* p. 3.
24. Ralph Nader, "Action For a Change," *The Consumer and Corporate Accountability,* p. 370.
25. Ralph Nader, "An Anatomy of Whistle Blowing," in *Whistle Blowing: The Report of the Conference For Professional Responsibility,* p. 7.
26. *Ibid.,* p. 3.

27. Ralph Nader, "Corporate Violence Against the Consumer," *The Rape of the Powerless,* p. 31.
28. Ralph Nader, introduction to *A Public Citizen's Action Manual,* by Donald Ross (New York: Grossman, 1973), p. viii.
29. *Ibid.*
30. *Congressional Quarterly Almanac,* 1974, p. 774; *Congressional Quarterly Almanac,* 1976, p. 283.
31. Garry Wills, "Hurrah for Politicians," p. 52.
32. *Ibid.*
33. Anthony Downs, *An Economic Theory of Democracy.*
34. John Schaar, "Power and Purity," p. 161.

Chapter Four. The Consumer in American Politics

1. Daniel R. Barney, *The Last Stand;* John C. Esposito, *Vanishing Air;* David Zwick and Marcy Benstock, *Water Wasteland.*
2. The plausibility of this assumption should not, however, be interpreted as a denial of Veblen's remark that many of us might sacrifice some of the so-called necessities of life in order to retain the proper degree of conspicuous consumption. Those of us who connect our identities to consumer satisfactions often do not make a priority ordering because the satisfaction of physical needs and the satisfaction of "extraneous desires" become almost one and the same.
3. E.F. Schumacher, "Buddhist Politics," quoted in *Toward A Steady State Economy,* ed. Herman Daly, p. 235.
4. Robert Heilbroner, *An Inquiry into the Human Prospect,* p. 88.
5. Robert Heilbroner and William Ophuls, *Ecology and the Politics of Scarcity;* Dennis Pirages and Paul Ehrlich, *Ark II.*
6. See Duncan MacRae, *The Social Function of Social Science* on the distinction between preferences and welfare. Good discussions of the public-interest concept can be found in: Brian Barry, *Political Argument;* Clarke Cochran, "Political Science and the 'Public Interest,' " pp. 327–55. William Connolly, "On 'Interests' in Politics", pp. 459–78; Richard Flathman, *The Public Interest;* Carl Friedrich, ed., *Nomos;* John S. Nelson, "Praxical Problems with Public-Interest Lobbies".
7. Connolly, pp. 455–56, quoting Brian Barry.
8. David Ignatius, "The Stages of Nader," 15 January, pp. 8ff
9. Peter Schuck, quoted in David Sanford, *Me and Ralph,* p. 49.
10. See Nelson, "Praxical Problems," pp. 35–44, for an insightful discussion of the distinction between citizens and consumers.
11. See Erving Goffman's chapter "Normal Appearances" in *Relations in Public* pp. 238–333 for the most vivid presentation of this perspective.
12. Simon Lazarus, *The Genteel Populists,* p. 150.
13. The best presentation of this argument is in Stuart Ewen, *Captains of Consciousness;* pp. 1–99. Also, John Kenneth Galbraith, *Economics and*

the Public Purpose, pp. 53–76, and Walter Weisskopf, "Economic
Growth vs. Existential Balance," in Daly, *Toward A Steady-State
Economy,* pp. 240–51.

14. Garry Wills, *Nixon Agonistes,* pp. 589–602.
15. A more extensive explication and critique in political ecology is found in
Chapter Six.
16. William Ophuls, "Leviathan or Oblivion," in Daly, *Toward A Steady-State
Economy,* p. 222.
17. Ophuls, *Ecology and the Politics of Scarcity,* p. 190.
18. Ophuls, *Ecology and the Politics of Scarcity,* p. 190.
19. Kenneth Boulding, quoted in Ophuls, "Leviathan or Oblivion," in Daly,
Toward a Steady-State Economy, p. 223.
20. Ophuls, "Leviathan or Oblivion," in Daly, *Toward A Steady-State Economy,*
p. 224.
21. Ophuls, "Leviathan or Oblivion," in Daly, *Toward A Steady-State Economy,*
pp. 226–29.
22. Robert Heilbroner, "The Political Dimension and 'Human Nature,' " in
An Inquiry into the Human Prospect, pp. 99–126.
23. Hannah Arendt, *The Human Condition* and Sheldon Wolin, *Politics and
Vision.*

Chapter Five. Our First Crisis of Affluence

1. Daniel M. Fox, *The Discovery of Abundance,* pp. 1–12.
2. *Ibid.*
3. Simon N. Patten, *Heredity and Social Progress* and *The Social Basis of
Religion.*
4. Simon N. Patten, *The Premises of Political Economy,* p. 1£.
5. Simon N. Patten, *The Consumption of Wealth,* p. 10.
6. *Ibid.*
7. *Ibid.,* p. 18.
8. *Ibid.,* p. 68.
9. *Ibid.*
10. *Ibid.,* p. 34.
11. Simon N. Patten, "Can Economics Furnish an Objective Standard for Morality," in *Essays In Economic Theory,* p. 140.
12. Simon N. Pattern, "The Economic Causes of Moral Progress" in *Essays in
Economic Theory,* p. 173.
13. *Ibid.,* p. 174.
14. *Ibid.,* p. 177.
15. *Ibid.,* p. 62.
16. Simon N. Patten, *The Consumption of Wealth,* p. 44.
17. *Ibid.,* p. 70.
18. *Ibid.,* pp. 68–69.
19. Simon N. Patten, "The Reconstruction of Economic Theory," in *Essays in
Economic Theory,* p. 286.
20. *Ibid.,* p. 280.

21. *Ibid.,* p. 323.
22. Fox, *The Discovery of Abundance,* pp. 32–43.
23. Thorstein Veblen, Review of Patten's *The Development of English Thought:* in *Essays, Reviews and Reports,* p. 554.
24. *Ibid.,* pp. 554–55.
25. *Ibid.,* p. 556.
26. *Ibid.,* p. 557.
27. Thorstein Veblen, *The Theory of the Leisure Class,* p. 81.
28. *Ibid.,* p. 102.
29. Thorstein Veblen, *Absentee Ownership and Business Enterprise in Recent Times,* p. 312.
30. *Ibid.,* p. 313.
31. *Ibid.,* p. 306.
32. Thorstein Veblen, *The Engineers and the Price System,* p. 109.
33. *Ibid.,* p. 8.
34. *Ibid.,* p. 28.
35. *Ibid.,* p. 41.
36. *Ibid.*
37. *Ibid.,* p. 55.
38. Thorstein Veblen, *The Vested Interests and the Common Man,* p. 30.
39. *Ibid.,* p. 163.
40. Thorstein Veblen, *The Engineers and the Price System,* p. 74.
41. *Ibid.,* p. 79.
42. Thorstein Veblen, *The Vested Interests and the Common Man,* p. 165.
43. Thorstein Veblen, *The Engineers and the Price System,* pp. 133–34.
44. *Ibid.,* p. 167.
45. Thorstein Veblen, *The Engineers and the Price System,* p. 167.
46. Thorstein Veblen, *The Instinct of Workmanship,* p. 34.

Chapter Six. Recycling Hobbes: The Limits to Political Ecology.

1. This perspective is evidenced in: Robert Heilbroner, *An Inquiry into the Human Prospect;* William Ophuls, *Ecology and the Politics of Scarcity;* Dennis Pirages and Paul Ehrlich, *Ark II.*
2. *Ibid.*
3. I'm not saying that public policy analysts are overtly nondemocratic but that the assumptions and methods of their discipline frequently lead them to see ecological problems as issues to be solved by better management and regulation. The best explication of the ideological assumptions rooted in the epistemology of policy analysis is Laurence Tribe, "Policy Science as Ideology," p. 66.
4. Other examples of nonindustrial ecological disorders can be found in Pierre Gounou, *The Tropical World: Its Social and Economic Conditions.* The more sensitive political ecologists do certainly recognize this.

5. James Ridgeway, *The Politics of Ecology.*

6. Hans Magnus Enzensberger, "Critique of Political Ecology," pp. 3–32.

7. *Ibid.*

8. An example of this can be seen in Fred Bossleman, "Ecology vs. Equality, the Sierra Club Meets the NAACP," pp. 93–95.

9. Enzensberger, "Critique of Political Ecology," p. 21.

10. Johan Galtung, "Limits to Growth and Class Politics," pp. 100–114.

11. Thomas Havener, "Democracy and Demography."

12. See Robert W. Tucker, "Egalitarianism and International Politics," pp. 27ff for an argument that runs contrary to mine.

13. The political realism of most coercive ecological solutions is questioned by Peter G. Stillman, "Ecological Problems, Political Theory, and Public Policy," in *Environmental Politics,* ed. Stuart Nagel, pp. 49–60.

14. Pirages and Ehrlich, *Ark II,* p. 130.

15. This is not to say that most social scientists currently do this kind of work. It is to note one manner in which they have dealt with the intricate problem of deciding where "values" should enter their analysis. See Arnold Brecht, *Political Theory.*

16. Paul Kress, "Politics and Science: A Contemporary View of an Ancient Association," pp. 1–13.

17. Sheldon Wolin, *Hobbes and the Epic Tradition of Political Theory.*

18. Pirages and Ehrlich, *Ark II,* pp. 164–65.

19. William Ophuls, "Reversal is the Law of Tao: The Imminent Resurrection of Political Philosophy," in *Environmental Politics,* ed. Nagel, p. 40.

20. In this respect, Marshall Berman has been our best chronicler of the sixties. See his "Sympathy for the Devil: Faust, the Sixties, and the Tragedy of Development," pp. 23–75 and "Buildings are Judgement or 'What Man Can Build,' " pp. 38ff.

21. This description of the sixties is suggested by John Schaar, in "Power and Purity," pp. 152–79.

22. For example, Peter Roberts, "The World Can Yet Be Saved," pp. 56–59; Wilfred Beckerman, *In Defense of Economic Growth.*

23. Enzensberger, "Critique of Political Ecology," p. 4.

24. See Mark Gavre, "Hobbes and His Audience," pp. 1544–56, for an explanation of how Hobbes' "Puritan argument" attempted to make his authoritarian solution appear reasonable to a significant portion of his audience.

25. Garrett Hardin, "The Tragedy of the Commons" in *Toward A Steady-State Economy,* ed. Herman Daly, p. 147.

26. *Ibid.,* p. 138.

27. Ophuls, *Ecology and the Politics of Scarcity,* p. 154.

28. Heilbroner, *An Inquiry into the Human Prospect,* pp. 102–103.

29. *Ibid.,* p. 105.

30. *Ibid.,* p. 106–07.

31. *Ibid.,* p. 108.

32. *Ibid.,* p. 109.
33. *Ibid.,* p. 113–14.
34. *Ibid.,* pp. 114–16.

Chapter Seven. Frail Hopes

1. Stuart Hill and David Orr, "Leviathan, the Open Society and the Crisis of Ecology," pp. 457–69.
2. *Congressional Quarterly Almanac,* 1971, p. 222.
3. Volkmar Lauber, "The Economic Growth Controversy in France."
4. Michael Walzer, "Politics in the Welfare State," p. 37.
5. *Ibid.,* p. 33.
6. This suggestion about the underside of the welfare state has been echoed by a number of neo-Marxist commentators. It has been even argued that the welfare state is primarily a political mechanism for employing members of the middle-class while maintaining the poor in a subordinate position.
7. Walzer, p. 29.
8. *Ibid.,* p. 34.
9. *Ibid.,* p. 35.
10. *Ibid.,* p. 37.
11. *Ibid.*
12. Ken Bode, "Discontent in Denver," p. 15.
13. *Ibid.*
14. Hugh Stretton, *Capitalism, Socialism and the Environment,* p. 314.

Bibliography

Books and Monographs

Arendt, Hannah. *The Human Condition.* New York: Doubleday Anchor, 1960.

Bachrach, Peter. *The Theory of Democratic Elitism: A Critique.* Boston: Little, Brown and Company, 1967.

Bachrach, Peter and Morton Baratz. *Power and Poverty: Theory and Practice.* New York: Oxford University Press, 1970.

Barney, Daniel R. *The Last Stand: Ralph Nader's Study Group Report on the National Forests.* New York: Grossman Publishers, 1974.

Barry, Brian. *Political Argument.* London: Routledge and K. Paul, 1965.

Beckerman, Wilfred. *In Defense of Economic Growth.* London: Jonathan Cape, 1974.

Benstock, Marcy and David Zwick. *Water Wasteland: Ralph Nader's Study Group Report on Water Pollution.* New York: Grossman Publishers, 1971.

Berry, Jeffrey. *Lobbying for the People.* Princeton: Princeton University Press, 1977.

Boorstin, Daniel J. *The Americans: The Democratic Experience.* New York: Random House, 1973.

Braverman, Harry. *Labor and Monopoly Capital: The Degradation of Work in the Twentieth Century.* New York: Monthly Review Press, 1975.

Brecht, Arnold. *Political Theory: The Foundations of Twentieth Century Political Thought.* Princeton: Princeton University Press, 1959.

Buckhorn, Robert. *Nader: The People's Lawyer.* Englewood Cliffs, N.J.: Prentice-Hall, 1972.

Connolly, William E., ed. *The Bias of Pluralism,* New York: Atherton Press, 1969.

Creighton, Lucy. *Pretenders to the Throne.* Lexington, Mass.: D.C. Heath, 1976.

Daly, Herman E. *Steady-State Economics; The Economics of Biophysical Equilibrium and Moral Growth,* San Francisco: W.H. Freeman, 1977.

Daly, Herman E., ed. *Toward A Steady-State Economy.* San Francisco: W.H. Freeman Company, 1973.

De Toledano, Ralph. *Hit and Run: The Rise and Fall?—of Ralph Nader.* New Rochelle, N.Y.: Arlington House, 1975.

Diggins, John P. *The Bard of Savagery: Thorstein Veblen and Modern Social Theory*. New York: Seabury, 1978.

Dorfman, Joseph. *Thorstein Veblen and His America*. New York: A.M. Kelley, 1966.

Dowd, Douglas. *Thorstein Veblen: A Critical Reappraisal*. Ithaca, N.Y.: Cornell University Press, 1958.

_____. *Thorstein Veblen*. New York: Washington Square Press, 1966.

Edelman, Murray, *The Symbolic Uses of Politics*. Urbana-Champaign: University of Illinois Press, 1964.

Ehrlich, Paul and Dennis Pirages. *Ark II: Social Responses to Environmental Imperatives*. San Francisco: W.H. Freeman Company, 1974.

Ellul, Jacques. *The Technological Society*. New York: Knopf, 1967.

Esposito, John C., director and Larry J. Silverman, associate director. *Vanishing Air: The Ralph Nader Study Group Report on Air Pollution*. New York: Grossman, 1970.

Ewen, Stuart. *Captains of Consciousness: Advertising and the Social Roots of the Consumer Culture*. New York: McGraw-Hill, 1976.

Fallows, James, Mark Green, and David Zwick. *Who Runs Congress?* New York: Bantam Books, 1972.

Fellmeth, Robert C., director. *The Interstate Commerce Commision, The Public Interest and the ICC: The Ralph Nader Study Group Report on the Interstate Commerce Commission and Transportation*. New York: Grossman Publishers, 1970.

Ferkiss, Victor C. *The Future of Technological Civilization*. New York: George Braziller, 1974.

Flatham, Richard. *The Public Interest: An Essay Concerning Normative Discourse*. New York: Wiley, 1966.

Fox, Daniel M. *The Discovery of Abundance: Simon N. Patten and the Transformation of Social Theory*. Ithaca: N.Y.: Cornell University Press, 1967.

Friedrich, Carl, ed. *Nomos V, The Public Interest*. New York: Atherton Press, 1962.

Galbraith, John Kenneth. *The Affluent Society* (2nd ed.). Boston: Houghton Mifflin, 1969.

_____. *Economics and the Public Purpose*. Boston: Houghton Mifflin, 1973.

_____. *The New Industrial State*. Boston: Houghton Mifflin, 1967.

Goffman, Erving. *Relations In Public: Microstudies of the Public Order*. New York: Basic Books, 1971.

Gorey, Hays. *Nader and the Power of Everyman*. New York: Grosset and Dunlap, 1975.

Gounou, Pierre. *The Tropical World: Its Social and Economic Conditions*. Translated by E.D. Laborde. New York: J. Wiley, 1961.

Green, Mark, with Beverly C. Moore and Bruce Wassersteing. *The Closed Enterprise System: Ralph Nader's Study Group Report on Anti-trust Enforcement*. New York: Grossman, 1972.

Green, Mark. *The Other Government: The Unseen Power of Washington Law-yers.* New York: Grossman Publishers, 1975.

Green, Mark J., ed., *The Monopoly Makers: Ralph Nader's Study Group Report on Regulation and Competition,* New York: Grossman Publishers, 1973.

Green, Mark and Bruce Wasserstein, eds. *With Justice for Some: An Indictment of the Law By Young Advocates.* Boston: Beacon Press, 1972.

Habermas, Jurgen. *Toward a Rational Society.* Translated by Jeremy Shapiro. Boston: Beacon Press, 1970.

Hardin, Garrett James. *Exploring New Ethics For Survival: The Voyage of the Spaceship Beagle.* New York: Viking Press, 1972.

_____. *The Limits of Altruism: An Ecologist's View of Survival.* Bloomington: Indiana University Press, 1977.

Hardin, Garrett and John Baden, eds. *Managing the Commons.* San Francisco: W.H. Freeman Company, 1977.

Harrison, Gordon and Sanford Jaffe. *The Public-Interest Law Firm.* New York: Ford Foundation, 1973.

Heilbroner, Robert. *An Inquiry into the Human Prospect.* New York: Norton, 1974.

Held, Virginia. *The Public-Interest and Individual Interests.* New York: Basic Books, 1970.

Jaffe, Sanford, *Public Interest Law: Five Years Later.* New York: Ford Foundation/American Bar Association, 1976.

James, Marlisle. *The People's Lawyers.* New York: Holt, Rhinehart and Winston, 1973.

Kariel, Henry. *Beyond Liberalism, Where Relations Grow.* San Francisco: Chandler and Sharp, 1977.

_____. *The Decline of American Pluralism.* Stanford: Stanford University Press, 1961.

Kariel, Henry, ed. *Frontiers of Democratic Theory.* New York: Random House, 1970.

Lauber, Volkmar. "The Economic Growth Controversy in France." Unpublished Ph.D. dissertation, University of North Carolina, Political Science Department, 1976.

Layton, Edwin T. *The Revolt of the Engineers: Social Responsibility and the American Engineering Profession.* Cleveland: Press of Case Western Reserve University, 1971.

Lazarus, Simon. *The Genteel Populists.* New York: Holt, Rhinehart, and Winston, 1974.

Leiss, William. *The Domination of Nature.* New York: George Braziller, 1972.

_____. *The Limits to Satisfaction: An Essay on the Problem of Needs and Commodities.* Toronto: University of Toronto Press, 1976.

Linder, Steffan. *The Harried Leisure Class.* New York: Columbia University Press, 1970.

McCarry, Charles. *Citizen Nader.* New York: Saturday Review Press, 1972.

McConnell, Grant. *Private Power and American Democracy.* New York: Vintage Books, 1966.

McFarland, Andrew S. *Public-Interest Lobbies: Decision-Making on Energy.* Washington, D.C.: American Enterprise Institute, 1976.

MacPherson, C.B. *The Life and Times of Liberal Democracy.* New York: Oxford University Press, 1977.

MacRae, Duncan. *The Social Function of Social Science.* New Haven: Yale University Press, 1976.

Marcuse, Herbert. *An Essay on Liberation.* Boston: Beacon Press, 1969.

_____. *One-Dimensional Man: Studies in the Ideology of Advanced Industrial Society.* Boston: Beacon Press, 1964.

Miroff, Bruce. *Pragmatic Illusions: The Presidential Politics of John F. Kennedy.* New York: David McKay, 1976.

Nadel, Mark V. *The Politics of Consumer Protection.* Indianapolis: Bobbs-Merrill, 1971.

Nader, Ralph. *Ralph Nader Congress Project.* 9 volumes. Washington, D.C.: Grossman Publishers, 1972.

Nader, Ralph. *Unsafe At Any Speed: The Designed-In Dangers of the American Automobile.* New York: Grossman, 1965.

Nader, Ralph and Donald Ross. *Action For a Change: A Student Manual For Public Interest Organizing.* New York: Grossman Publishers, 1971.

Nader, Ralph and John Abbotts. *The Menace of Atomic Energy.* New York: Norton, 1977.

Nader, Ralph, Mark Green, and Joel Seligman. *Taming The Giant Corporation.* New York: Norton, 1976.

Nader, Ralph, ed. *The Consumer And Corporate Accountability.* New York: Harcourt, Brace, Jovanovich, 1973.

Nader, Ralph and Mark Green, eds. *Ralph Nader's Conference on Corporate Accountability.* New York: Grossman, 1973.

Nader, Ralph, Peter J. Petkas, and Kate Blackwell, eds. *Whistle Blowing: The Report of the Conference On Professional Responsibility.* New York: Grossman, 1972.

Nagel, Stuart S., ed. *Environmental Politics.* New York: Praeger, 1974.

Nisbet, Robert A. *A Quest For Community.* New York: Oxford University Press, 1970.

Nisbet, Robert A. *Twilight of Authority.* New York: Oxford University Press, 1975.

Noble, David F. *America By Design: Science, Technology and the Rise of Corporate Capitalism.* New York: Knopf, 1977.

Noble, David W. *The Paradox of Progressive Thought.* Minneapolis: University of Minnesota, 1958.

Olson, Mancur, Jr. *The Logic of Collective Action.* New York: Schocken, 1968.

Ophuls, William. *Ecology and the Politics of Scarcity.* San Francisco: W.H. Freeman Company, 1977.

Osborne, William, ed. *The Rape of the Powerless.* New York: Gordon and Breach, 1971.

Page, Joseph A. and Mary Win-O'Brien. *Bitter Wages: Ralph Nader's Study Group Report on Disease and Injury on the Job*. New York: Grossman Publishers, 1973.

Passmore, John. *Man's Responsibility For Nature*. London: Duckworth, 1974.

Patten, Simon N. *The Consumption of Wealth*. Philadelphia: University of Pennsylvania, 1901.

_____. *Essays In Economic Theory*. Edited by Rexford Tugwell. New York: Knopf, 1934.

Patten, Simon Nelson. *The New Basis of Civilization*. New York: The Macmillan Company, 1913.

_____. *The Premises of Poliical Economy*. New York: The Macmillan Company, 1966.

_____. *The Social Basis of Religion*. New York: 1911.

Piven, Frances Fox and Richard Cloward. *Regulating the Poor*. New York: Pantheon, 1971.

Ridgeway, James. *The Politics of Ecology*. New York: Dutton, 1970.

Riesman, David. *Thorstein Veblen: A Critical Interpretation*. New York: Seabury, 1975.

Sanford, David. *Me and Ralph: Is Nader Unsafe for America?* Washington: New Republic Books, 1976.

Schumacher, E.F. *Small Is Beautiful: Economics as if People Mattered*. New York: Harper and Row, 1973.

Stretton, Hugh. *Capitalism, Socialism and the Environment*. Cambridge, England: Cambridge University Press, 1976.

Veblen, Thorstein. *Absentee Ownership and Business Enterprise in Recent Times: The Case of America*. New York: A.M. Kelley, 1964.

_____. *The Engineers and the Price System*. New York: A.M. Kelley Publishers, 1965.

_____. *Essays in Our Changing Order*. New York: A.M. Kelley, 1964.

_____. *Essays, Reviews and Reports*. Edited by Joseph Dorfman. Clifton, N.J.: A.M. Kelley, 1973.

_____. *An Inquiry into the Nature of Peace and the Terms of Its Perpetuation*. New York: A.M. Kelley, 1964.

_____. *The Instinct of Workmanship*. New York: Macmillan Company, 1914.

_____. *The Theory of Business Enterprise*. New York: Charles Scribner's Sons, 1932.

_____. *The Theory of the Leisure Class*. New York: The Modern Library, 1934.

_____. *The Vested Interests and the Common Man*. New York: A.M. Kelley, 1964.

Whiteside, Thomas. *The Investigation of Ralph Nader: General Motors vs. One Determined Man*. New York: Arbor House, 1972.

Wills, Garry. *Nixon Agonistes: The Crisis of the Self-Made Man*. Boston: Houghton Mifflin, 1970.

Winner, Langdon. *Autonomous Technology: Technics Out-of-Control as a Theme in Political Thought*. Cambridge, Mass.: MIT Press, 1977.

Wolff, Robert Paul. *The Poverty of Liberalism*. Boston: Beacon Press, 1968.

Wolin, Sheldon S. *Hobbes and The Epic Tradition of Political Theory.* Los Angeles: William Allen Clark Memorial Library, University of California, 1970.

Wolin, Sheldon. *Politics and Vision: Continuity and Innovation in Western Political Thought.* Boston: Little, Brown and Company, 1960.

Articles and Unpublished Papers

Anderson, Patrick. "Ralph Nader, Crusader; or, The Rise of a Self-Appointed Lobbyist." *The New York Times Magazine,* 29 October 1967, pp.25ff.

Armstrong, Richard. "The Passion That Rules Ralph Nader." *Fortune,* May 1971, pp. 144ff.

Auerbach, Carl. "Some Comments on Mr. Nader's Views." *Minnesota Law Review* 54, (1970), pp. 503–08.

Berman, Marshall. "Sympathy for the Devil: Faust, the Sixties and the Tragedy of Development." *American Review* 19, January 1974, pp. 23–75.

_____. "Buildings Are Judgement or 'What Man Can Build.' " *Ramparts,* March, 1975, pp. 33ff.

Bode, Ken. "Discontent In Denver." *The New Republic,* 23 July 1977, pp. 14–17.

Boffey, P.M. "Nader's Raiders and the FDA: Science and Scientists Misused." *Science,* 17 April 1970, pp. 349–52.

_____. "Nader and the Scientists: A Call For Responsibility." *Science,* 12 February 1971, pp. 549–51.

Bossleman, Fred. "Ecology vs. Equality, The Sierra Club Meets the NAACP." *Yale Review of Law and Social Action,* 1971, pp. 93–95.

Brandon, H. "One Man Who Mattered." *Saturday Review,* 28 May 1966, pp. 9–10.

Burlingham, Bo. "Popular Politics: The Arrival of Ralph Nader." *Working Papers For A New Society,* Summer 1974, pp. 5–14.

Carter, Luther J. "Campaign G.M.: Corporation Critics Seek Support of Universities." *Science,* 24 April 1970, pp. 452–55.

Chamberlain, John. "Auto Safety, The Truth and the Hokum." *National Review,* 4 April 1967, pp. 343–46.

Cochran, Clarke E. "Political Science and the 'Public Interest'." *Journal of Politics* 36, May 1974, pp. 327–55.

Cohen, Richard E. "Drive Launched to Require U.S. Charters for Major Companies." *National Journal Reports,* 12 April 1975, pp. 549–51.

Connolly, William C. "On 'Interests' In Politics." *Politics And Society,* Summer, 1977, pp. 459–78.

DeBaggio, T. "Gadfly in Carpet Slippers." *The Nation,* 8 May 1972, pp. 597–98.

Duscha, J. "Stop! In the Public Interest!" *The New York Times Magazine,* 21 March 1971, pp. 4ff.

Enzensberger, Hans Magnus. "Critique of Political Ecology." *New Left Review,* March-April 1974, pp. 3–32.

Ferre', Frederick. "Hope and Myth in a World of Scarcity." *The Georgia Review* 32, Fall 1978, pp. 553–70.

Fromm, Harold. "From Transcendence to Obsolence: A Route Map." *The Georgia Review* 32, Fall 1978, pp. 543–52.

Galtung, Johan. "Limits to Growth and Class Politics." *Journal of Peace Research* 10, no. 1 (1973): 100–14.

Gavre, Mark. "Hobbes and His Audience: The Dynamics of Theorizing." *American Political Science Review,* December 1974, pp. 1544–56.

Golden, L. "G.M. and Harassment." *Saturday Review,* 13 August 1966, p. 56.

Havener, Thomas. "Democracy And Demography." Southern Peace Science Association Meetings, April 1975.

Herrmann, Robert O. and Warland Rex. "Nader's Support: Its Sources And Concerns." *Journal of Consumer Affairs,* Summer 1976, pp. 1–18.

Hill, Stuart and David Orr. "Leviathan, The Open Society and the Crisis of Ecology." *The Western Political Quarterly,* December 1978, pp. 457–69.

Holden, C. "Nader Group Sees Water Wasteland." *Science,* 30 April 1971, p. 455.

———. "Nader On Mental Health Centers, A Movement That Got Bogged Down." *Science,* 4 August 1972, pp. 413–15.

Ignatius, David. "The Stages of Nader." *The New York Times Sunday Magazine,* 15 January 1976, pp. 8ff.

Ingram, T.H. "Corporate Underground." *The Nation,* 13 September 1971, pp. 206–212.

"Interview with Ralph Nader: A Progress Report on Consumer Issues." *U.S. News and World Report,* 27 October 1975, p. 26.

"Is Nader Losing His Clout." *U.S. News and World Report,* 19 December 1977, p. 18.

Jacqueney, Theodore. "Nader Network Switches Focus to Legal Action, Congressional Lobbying." *National Journal Reports,* 9 June 1973, pp. 840–49.

Klein, Joe. "Ralph Nader: The Rolling Stone Interview." *Rolling Stone,* 20 November 1975, pp. 54ff.

Kress, Paul. "Politics and Science: A Contemporary View of an Ancient Association." *Polity* 2, (1969), pp. 1–13.

Langer, E. "Auto Safety: Nader vs. General Motors." *Science,* 1 April 1966, pp. 47–50.

Leone, R.C. "Public-Interest Advocacy and the Regulatory Process." *The Annals of the American Academy,* March 1972, pp. 46–58.

Leventhal, Paul L. "Political Reaction Overshadows Reform Aim of Massive Nader Congress Study." *National Journal Reports,* 23 September 1972, pp. 1483–95.

Marshall, Eliot. "St. Nader and His Evangelists." *The New Republic,* 23 October 1971, p. 13.

"Meet Ralph Nader." *Newsweek,* 22 January 1968, pp. 65–67.

"Milk Money." *The New Republic,* 12 February 1972, p. 7.

Millen, Steve. "Ralph Nader's Consumer Populism." *International Socialist Review,* May 1973, pp. 6–9.

"Muckraking, 1966." *The Nation,* 21 March 1966, p. 316.

Mueller, Marti. "Nader: From Auto Safety to a Permanent Crusade." *Science,* 21 November 1969, pp. 979–83.

Nader, Ralph. "Profits vs. Engineering: The Corvair Story; exerpts from *Unsafe At Any Speed." The Nation,* 1 November 1965, pp. 295–301.

_____. "Safer Cars: Time for Decision." *Consumer Reports,* April 1966, pp. 1934–97.

_____. "Seven Safety Features Cars Need Most." *Science Digest,* August 1966, pp. 75–79.

_____. "Business Crime." *The New Republic,* 9 September 1967, pp. 7–8.

_____. "Inventions and Their Uses." *The New Republic,* 22 July 1967, pp. 32–34.

_____. "Watch That Hamburger." *The New Republic,* 19 August 1967, pp. 15–16.

_____. "We're Still In The Jungle." *The New Republic,* 15 July 1967, pp. 11–12.

_____. "X-ray Exposures." *The New Republic,* 2 September 1967, pp. 11–12.

_____. "Something Fishy." *The New Republic,* 6 January 1968, pp. 19–21.

_____. "Infernal, External, Internal Combustion Engine." *The New Republic,* 27 April 1968, pp. 7–8.

_____. "Lo, The Poor Indian." *The New Republic,* 30 March 1968, pp. 14–15.

_____. "They're Still Breathing." *The New Republic,* 3 February 1968, p. 15.

_____. "Wake-up America, Unsafe X-rays." *Ladies Home Journal,* May 1968, pp. 126–27.

Nader, Ralph and Jerome Gordon. "Safety On The Job." *The New Republic,* 15 June 1968, pp. 23–25.

Nader, Ralph. "Danger in Toyland." *Ladies Home Journal,* November 1969, pp. 81ff.

_____. "Law Schools, Law Firms." *The New Republic,* 11 October 1969, pp. 20–23.

_____. "Swiss Cheese." *The New Republic,* 22 November 1969, pp. 11–12.

_____. "Baby Foods, Can You (and your baby) Afford Them?" *McCalls,* November 1970, pp. 36ff.

_____. "Yablonski's Unfinished Business." *The Nation,* 26 January 1970, pp. 70–72.

_____. "Burned Children." *The New Republic,* 3 July 1971, pp. 19–21.

_____. "Cotton-Mill Killer." *The Nation,* 15 March 1971, pp. 335–37.

_____. "Dossier Invades The Homes." *Saturday Review,* 17 April 1971, pp. 18–21.

_____. "Making Congress Work." *The New Republic,* 21 August 1971, pp. 19–21.

_____. "Mr. Nixon's Tricky Bonanza." *The Nation,* 21 June 1971, pp. 774–76.

_____. "New Dimensions in Citizenship." *PTA Magazine,* October 1971, pp. 17–21.

_____. "We Need a New Kind of Patriotism." *Life,* 9 July 1971, p. 4.

_____. "How You Lose Your Money by Being a Woman." *McCalls,* January, 1972, pp. 65ff.

_____. "Home, Unsafe Home." *Ladies Home Journal,* January 1972, pp. 70ff.

_____. "In The Public Interest." *New Republic,* (February 19, March 4, March 11, March 18, April 8, April 15, May 27, August 19, December 2, 1972).

_____. "Ralph Nader Reports." *Ladies Home Journal,* (February, March, April, May, June, July, August, September, October, November, December, 1972, January 1973).

_____. "Scientist and His Indentured Professional Societies." *Bulletin of Atomic Scientists,* February 1972, pp. 43–44.

Nader, Ralph and M. Green, *"Crime in the Suites." The New Republic,* 29 April 1972, pp. 17–18.

Nader, Ralph and T. Stanton. "Our Tax Laws Favor the Rich and Complexity Makes It Worse." *Saturday Review,* 21 October 1972, p. 46.

"Nader Look." *The New Republic,* 22 July 1972, p. 10.

"Nader's Neophytes." *Time,* 13 September 1968, p. 23.

Nelson, John S. "Toltechs, Aztechts and the Art of the Possible." *Polity,* 8 (Fall, 1975), pp. 80–116.

_____. "Praxical Problems with Public-Interest Lobbies." Unpublished Paper, Department of Political Science, University of Iowa, 1977.

Newfield, Jack. "Nader's Raiders: The Lone Ranger Gets a Posse," *Life,* 3 October 1969, pp. 56ff.

Phillips, James G. "Nader, Nuclear Industry, Prepare to Battle Over the Atom." *National Journal Reports,* 1 February 1975, pp. 153–64.

Posner, Richard. "Nader on Anti-trust." *The New Republic,* 26 June 1971, pp. 11–14.

"Public-Interest Lobbies: Nader and Common Cause Become Permanent Fixtures." *Congressional Quarterly Weekly Reports,* 15 May 1976, pp. 1197–1205.

"Ralph Nader Takes on Congress as Well as Big Business." *National Journal Reports,* 11 March 1978, pp. 388–90.

Ridgeway, James. "Dick." *The New Republic,* 12 March 1966, pp. 11–13.

_____. "G.M. Comes Clean." *The New Republic,* 2 April 1966, pp. 8–9.

Roberts, Peter. "The World Can Yet Be Saved." *New Scientist,* 9 January 1975, pp. 56–58.

"Sedulus," "Nader as Performer." *The New Republic,* 2 January 1971, pp. 40–42.

Tribe, Laurence, "Policy Science as Ideology," *Philosophy and Public Affairs* 2, no. 1 (1972), pp. 66–110.

Tucker, Robert W. "Egalitarianism and International Politics." *Commentary,* September 1975, pp. 27ff.

Vidal, Gore. "Best Man '72." *Esquire,* June 1971, pp. 102–05.

Wade, Nicholas. "Nader's Congress Project: Political Scientists Intrigued But Fretful." *Science,* 13 October 1972, pp. 142–46.

_____. "Nader's Profiles Aimed At Voters Not Headlines." *Science,* 27 October 1972, p. 382.

Watzman, S. "Nader's Raiders and the Traders." *The Nation,* 29 September 1969, p. 317.

Walzer, Michael. "Politics in the Welfare State." *Dissent,* January-February 1968, pp. 26–40.

"Who's Mr. Clean?" *The New Republic,* 1 May 1971, pp. 7–8.

Winter, Ralph K. "Economic Regulation vs. Competition: Ralph Nader and Creeping Capitalism." *Yale Law Journal* 82, (1973), pp. 890–902.

Young, L. "Chink in Nader's Armor?" *The New Republic,* 2 September 1972, p. 11.

Index